The Glass Walking-Stick

The Glass Walking-Stick

and

Other Essays

from

THE ILLUSTRATED LONDON NEWS
1905-1936

by

G. K. CHESTERTON

Edited by

DOROTHY COLLINS

with a Preface by

ARTHUR BRYANT

METHUEN & CO. LTD, LONDON
36 *Essex Street, Strand,* WC2

First published in 1955

REF
PR
4453
.C4
A16
1955
Cop. 1

CATALOGUE NO. 5764/U

PRINTED AND BOUND IN GREAT BRITAIN BY
RICHARD CLAY AND COMPANY, LTD, BUNGAY, SUFFOLK

CONTENTS

Showing year of publication in the Illustrated London News

PREFACE

BY ARTHUR BRYANT

GILBERT KEITH CHESTERTON spent his whole life in teaching others how to live. Even today the sound of his name is like a trumpet-call. To him the world was a field in which one went about doing battle with evil in order that good might endure. If from his generation one had to select the name of one man who might have stood as type of Don Quixote or St George who slew the dragon, it was he. If any literary name of our age becomes a legend transcending letters, it will, I believe, be his. In his lifetime he was often likened to Dr Johnson, and it was an analogy that did not only depend on his giant girth and splendid conversation. For like Johnson he never penned a line or uttered a sentence that harboured a mean or ignoble thought, nor did he ever miss an opportunity of striking a blow for what he felt to be right. In all that he did and stood for there was neither fear nor calculation. He was the kind of man of whom Bunyan was thinking when he drew the picture of Mr Greatheart. His sword was at the service of pilgrims.

And what a sword it was! It is nearly half a century now since, in his dedication to 'The Man Who was Thursday', he roused the heart of a new generation to challenge the cold decadence of an unbelieving and selfish intellectualism:

A cloud was on the mind of men, and wailing went the weather,
Yea, a sick cloud upon the soul when we were boys together.
Science announced nonentity and art admired decay;

The world was old and ended : but you and I were gay.
Round us in antic order their crippled vices came—
Lust that had lost its laughter, fear that had lost its shame.

Looking back on it, we can still feel the fire of that
protest, even as he felt it when, as a boy, he first opened
Stevenson's book, and—

. . . cool and clear and sudden as a bird sings in the grey,
Dunedin to Samoa spoke, and darkness unto day.
But we were young; we lived to see God break their bitter
   charms,
God and the good Republic come riding back in arms :
We have seen the city of Mansoul, even as it rocked,
   relieved—
Blessed are they who did not see, but being blind, believed.

It was the greatness of Chesterton's creed that the
salvation he preached was the salvation not of the elect,
but of the many. His concern was always with the common man. He did not confine his sympathies to the well-
behaved and refined : to the recluse in the cloister or the
scholar in the study. He was not one of those who thought
that only the best were to be saved; his catholicism was
an all-comprehending democracy. And it was one that
was founded on a deep understanding of all that
humanity needs; not only of its sufferings but of its joys.
He did not only wish to shelter the oppressed from the
clouds that threatened them, but wished also to see them
rejoicing in the sunshine. He was the champion of all
those things that make common men happy—of laughter
and marriage, of home and beer. Like old Samuel Johnson, he loved the poor, not with the perfunctory pity of
the professional philanthropist, but with an earnest desire
to make them as uproariously happy as he himself was
happy. That was why he so admired Dickens, the poet
in excelsis of the joys and humours of plain, suffering,

unvarnished humanity. Yet, though his inferior in sheer creative genius, he had nothing of the egotism and self-pity of Dickens. He was too good for that. I never met a more generous man, and I never saw a happier. I do not believe there is anyone who had the inestimable privilege of knowing Gilbert Keith Chesterton who would not say the same.

We live in a Protestant country and are a Protestant people, and Chesterton, in the latter years of his life, was a Roman Catholic. Having begun his career in a blaze of early triumph and popularity such as comes to few men, he put it by him and set his face against the stream of contemporary thought. Whether one agrees or not with his choice of Faith and Dogma, there is not the least question that in doing so he singled out for attack many elements in our modern civilization which are both powerful and intolerant of criticism, even when the attack was as good-humoured and full of healthy laughter as his always was. He did not thereby make his task any the easier. For ephemeral reasons, though for no others, his influence in his lifetime was therefore limited. Yet by virtue of this very fact, I believe his influence on unborn generations will be the greater. For though his public at the end of his career was probably smaller than at its triumphant beginning, it was a public that counted for more.   It was the kind of public that read his books not merely for pleasure and amusement but because it found in them a faith and an inspiration. That faith and inspira-tion is not diminished now that he is dead, and it will continue to be transmitted to others. And his books will continue to be read, and, I think, increasingly read.

For ninety-nine people out of a hundred, perhaps for nine hundred and ninety-nine out of a thousand, life tends to be a dull and uninspired affair, a round of

prosaic duties which are got through for some ulterior
end and without joy or relish in the performance. It was
Chesterton's supreme merit that he never saw life or
presented it to others as anything but a flaming and
glorious romance. He did so, without any attempt to over-
look its material aspects; on the contrary, he emphasized
these and saw in them the complete justification of his
creed. The very weakness of man was to him something
to be rejoiced over and turned to good account. 'When
Christ', he once wrote, 'at a symbolic moment was
establishing His great society, He chose for its corner-stone
neither the brilliant Paul nor the mystic John, but a
shuffler, a snob, a coward—in a word, a man. And upon
this rock He has built His church, and the gates of Hell
have not prevailed against it. All the empires and the
kingdoms have failed, because of this inherent and con-
tinual weakness, that they were founded by strong men
and upon strong men. But this one thing, the historic
Christian Church, was founded on a weak man, and for
that reason it is indestructible.' Chesterton followed a
Master who was born in a peasant's manger and died on
a rough-hewn cross. And like Him he knew that in these
plain and unadorned instruments of common life were
the chains of Hell and the keys of Heaven, angels ascend-
ing and descending, and the son of man glorified.

THE GLASS WALKING-STICK

PRACTICAL politics are in this world continually coming to grief; for the truth is that practical politics are too practical for this world. This world is so incurably romantic that things never work out properly if you base them on the sound business principle. For instance, it is always assumed in modern social philosophy that ornaments, curiosities, *objets d'art,* etc., are things that people add to their lives when they have procured all that is solid and sensible. The actual fact is quite otherwise. The savage wears an *objet d'art* in his nose before he discovers that clothes are of any use at all. Man discovered that dress was a luxury before he discovered that dress was a necessity. It is not only true that luxuries are more noble than necessities; it really seems as if they were more necessary than necessities.

I see that the vicar of a very poor district has made an experiment of quite extraordinary interest. He suggested that the poor should bring out all the objects of interest that they had in their houses; and he undertook to see that they got the best possible price for them, if they cared to sell. There is a wonderful irony and significance about his offer. He asked the poor to produce expensive things; and they did. He demanded diamonds, so to speak, from the men who had no bread. He asked the starving what treasure was hidden in their houses. He knew human nature. The incredible fact fell out exactly in accordance with his demand. The people who could hardly keep the rags together on their backs brought out of their houses things which were not only genuinely worth study, but

I

were genuinely worth money. They were all curiosities, numbers of them were expensive curiosities. Several of them had that unique quality which more than either use or beauty draws out money in torrents and maddens the hearts of millionaires. One poor woman, for instance, had a patchwork quilt made out of fragments of the French and English uniforms at Waterloo. Words are absolutely inadequate to express the poetry of such a quilt as that; to express all that is involved in the colours of that strange reconciliation. The hope and hunger of the great Revolution, the legend of isolated France, the starry madness of the Man of Destiny, the nations of chivalry that he conquered, the nation of shopkeepers that he did not conquer, their long and dull defiance, the lost agony of Europe at war with a man, the fall that was like the fall of Lucifer—all those things were on that poor old woman's quilt, and every night she drew over her poor old bones the heraldry of a thousand heroes. On her coverlet two terrific nations were at peace at last. That quilt ought to be strung up on to a great pole and carried in front of King Edward and the French President in every celebration of the *Entente Cordiale*. But a poor householder owned it and never thought of its value.

The other exhibits had, in one way or another, this same quaint and picturesque and unexpected character. One man had a walking-stick made of glass and filled with sweets. If there were children in the house, the preservation of that glass stick has something of the insane sublimity of a religion. Many had weapons of undoubted antiquity. Several had weapons with definite and ascertainable historical associations. A boot of the Duke of Marlborough was (I think) one of the exhibits. I do not know how this boot became detached from its fellow; but when I recall the clear intellect and fine financial genius of the Conqueror of Blenheim, together with that liberal disdain of the pedantries of personal dignity which also distinguished him—in short, when I reconstruct the whole moral character of Marlborough, I think it highly probable that he sold one of his boots for threepence and hopped home. Another of the vicar's parishioners had an old picture of the Flood, so old that quite competent authorities described it literally as 'priceless'. I do not know how old this picture of the Flood really was; but it is a mere matter of fact that the owner received for it a sum such as he had never seen in his life. Yet he had let the thing hang on his walls quite undisturbed probably through many periods of acute economic distress. Some of the exhibits were entirely wild and odd; but I am not sure that I did not like them as well as any. One was a stuffed lamb with an unnatural number of heads or legs or something, which had really been born on some country estate. Simple and uneducated people have no horror of physical monstrosities; just as educated people have no horror of moral monstrosities. But the broad characteristic of all the things described was emphatically the fact that they were interesting things. And this is particularly a quality of them as things collected by the poor. The cultivated people go in for what is beautiful; but the uncultivated for what is interesting. For example, the more refined people concern themselves with literature—that is, with beautiful statements. But simple people concern themselves with scandal—that is, with interesting statements. Interest often exists apart from beauty; and interest is immeasurably better and more important than beauty. I myself know a man who is beautiful and remarkably uninteresting. The distinction is one that affects religion and morals and the practical philosophy of living. Existence often ceases to be beautiful; but if we are men at all it never ceases to be interesting. This divine creation in the midst of which we live does commonly, in the words of the good books, combine amusement with instruction. But dark hours will come when the wisest man can hardly get instruction out of it; but a brave man can always get amusement out of it. When we have given up valuing life for every other reason, we can still value it, like the glass stick, as a curiosity. For the universe is like the glass stick in this, at any rate; it is unique.

HISTORY IN STONE

THERE is a kind of war between bricks and books; I mean
between the tradition of materials and the tradition of
theories. In so many places the church contradicts the
parson and the castle contradicts the earl; the Parliament
says one thing and the parliament house another. Anyone
who has gone rambling in England must have noticed a
strange thing often only half perceived and generally
wholly unexplained. I mean the entire difference between
English history, especially early English history as it is in
the ordinary history books, and the same English history
in so far as it remains in buildings, in local customs, or in
popular associations in England. The old kings, bishops,
and soldiers seem to be entirely different people when
they appear in stone and when they appear in print. I do
not mean that the school histories are untrue; I do not
even mean that they contradict the other impressions or
are inconsistent with them in any particular. But the two
are two different worlds; in the second is revealed a whole
universe of interests and activities, about which the first
was literally deaf and dumb. It is as if we had heard of
Tennyson's peerage but never of his poetry; or as if we
had heard of Wellington's premiership but never of his
generalship; or as if a biographer of Columbus had been
explanatory about the egg but silent about the American
continent.

Let me take a typical example. The story of the dynastic violence of fifteenth-century England is, in the
school-books, really picturesque. We see the Lion of Agincourt dying with a doom upon his usurping house, leaving

all that it had gained in England to the intrigue and
audacity of Gloucester, all that it had gained in France
to the exterminating nationalism of Joan of Arc. The
only staff on which Lancaster can lean is King Harry's
daughter-in-law, Margaret of Anjou, a woman almost as
militant as Joan of Arc herself. Among these strong and
sinister figures, somewhat diseased but intensely dramatic,
one scarcely looks at the poor pale-faced lad, said not to
be quite right in his head, who actually inherits the
crowns of England and France. Battles are fought round
him, as round the wooden pole of a flagstaff; councils are
held round him, as round the dead mace on the table of
Parliament. He always seems to be locked up somewhere
and forgotten; and we do not even remember his foolish
face as we watch Margaret defying the outlaws in the
forest, or Richard Crookback red with the rout of Tewkesbury. We scarcely know when he dies. His murder is
quieter than most men's natural deaths. That is how King
Henry VI appears in the written English histories—or
rather how he does not appear. It bears no resemblance,
it contains no hint of how he still appears, not in English
histories, but in England. I do not mean that his character
appears particularly different; I mean that one discovers
a new field of activity for such a character. It is not that the
face or figure of the feeble youth is contradicted—it is as
if we walked into fairyland, where such a youth may gain
all the omnipotence of the fairies. It is like finding that a
housemaid is a medium or the village idiot a magician.

Walk westward out of London along the Valley of the
Thames and you will find a huge educational foundation
which has passed almost into a synonym for the British
Empire and the aristocracy that administers that Empire.
It is enormously wealthy; it is enormously powerful; it is
known all over the world as much, or more, than Oxford

or Cambridge; and every boy or man who has anything
to do with it is reminded morning and evening in all the
prayers and ceremonies of the place that the wealth and
power by which he lives is the wealth and power of King
Henry VI. The most successful of soldiers declares that he
won Waterloo by the influence that lost Tewkesbury. The
timid and impotent boy is still (even after a profound
change of religion) the patron saint and benefactor of
hundreds of the athletic or ambitious boys that make up
the great legend of Eton and the English public-schools.
Walk eastward out of London into the flat counties till
you come to one of the two Universities that are the two
fountains of the national life and letters. You will find one
College of which the chapel towers in beauty and tradition above all the roofs of that beautiful and traditional
town; the whole world of culture has come to it for its
architecture or its music or its stained glass. It is one of
the wonders of the English world. And there is not a
porter so ignorant nor an undergraduate so frivolous, that
he has not been told twenty times and repeated twenty
times that it is the half-witted Henry who through five
centuries sustains this palace of God. This weakest of
Kings is *the* King *par excellence,* for the place is called
'King's College', not King Henry's. The difference of impression is very strange; it is a difference, it is not a contradiction. Little of what the history-book says is untrue;
but the history-book says so little. Henry VI was not an
effective fighter or a sagacious statesman; and if we see
the Middle Ages as a gory tangle like Tewkesbury, we
shall see him as very small. But if we take a turn or two
down an English lane and see the Middle Ages as an
ancient and rich civilization, creative and systematic, with
fruitful sciences and masterful arts—then we shall see him
as gigantic.

B

Numerous other instances, of course, could be given. An intelligent boy reading at school of the quarrel between St Thomas Becket and Henry II naturally sympathizes, on the whole, with the latter : the King seems at worst an impatient man of action; the saint seems at best an aggravating sacerdotalist. Let the boy shut the History of England and open (let us say) the poems of Chaucer, written by an ordinary Englishman for Kings and Queens not so very long after the King was scourged in the cathedral. He will have great difficulty in making head or tail of the world in which he finds himself. He will find himself in medieval England in which every man, woman, and child utterly and entirely takes it for granted that St Thomas justly opposed the King, as utterly and entirely as that St George justly opposed the Dragon. The same bewildering impression which the boy would find in Chaucer he would also find in Canterbury. These atmospheres never depend upon any detail and are always impossible to describe; but he will feel the whole cathedral rising like one roar of unanimous assent, the very stones crying out that the blood of a just man was shed. These are things that modern books of history do not explain. You must steep yourself in the atmosphere of many old towns and old books before you begin to understand them.

So there hangs over all England this singular double impression of political history and of popular institution. Men who are remembered only for their cruelties in Hume or Hallam, are remembered only for their charities in Somerset or Sussex. From the marches of Scotland to the old kingdom of Cornwall, the English soil is loaded with the pieties of blasphemers, with the almsgiving of oppressors, with the ascetical enthusiasms of gluttons and drunkards, with the high artistic culture of barbarians. William

Rufus perished in Hampshire by his hunting, but he remains in Westminster by his building. Henry VII hammered together a huge machine of practical despotism; nothing remains of him but a chapel. It looks as if there were a whole aspect of the lives of these people that is perpetually overlooked in dealing with them; and, indeed, such an oversight is common enough in the criticism of human life. I fancy that we must begin to fill in these void places in history with the vivid, though visible, thoughts of the men that worked there; otherwise it will be like watching men dancing and not hearing the tune.

THE OLD NURSE

I was recently reading a very interesting study which set my thoughts rambling on many themes; and not least on the theme of old nurses. For many other reasons it should be of interest to English people; especially those of them who have had the rudimentary intelligence to be interested in Irish people. For it is clear that the memories with which the mind of this old nurse were filled, and almost choked, were the memories of the great Irish Famine, which she had known in her childhood and which she communicated so vividly to an American child. The Irish Famine was more than an earthquake; it was an explosion. As an explosion scatters the arms and legs of a single man, so this catastrophe scattered the separated parts of a single people; and that most tragically, before our own people had attempted any real justice to that people. For that reason, the ruin of Ireland simply strewed the whole earth with the enemies of England. What region in the world, cried the Trojan after the Fall of Troy, is not full of our ruin? What region in the world is not now full of that wrong which we remedied so late? The testimony of the old nurse in America is all the more forcible, because of the patient simplicity with which she narrated such wrongs. Nobody is blamed for an earthquake; and nobody is of necessity blamed for an explosion; but people are blamed for their conduct during an earthquake or after an explosion. And it is the ugly truth that the blight of the Famine was not merely a blight upon a particular order of vegetables; among the blighted, not to say the blighters, were to be found a higher order of animals; even including politicians. The old Irish nurse meekly witnessed to the wickedness of a neighbouring landlord who would not give food to starving men unless they were of his own faction. And everyone knows that a hundred juries handed down Lord John Russell as a murderer. For that part of the record alone it would have been well worth recording. But I confess that I was very much interested in this Irish-American nurse merely considered as a nurse. She was a pattern of that paradox of submission and supremacy which belonged to that sort of old-fashioned servant. And it set me thinking about something that was lost, when the nurse gave place to the governess and the governess gave place to the schoolmistress. Bad and good abound in both; but something organic gave place to something official.

What is the matter with English Education is that it is discussed in Educational English. Even criticisms of Education, even complaints of Education, even confessions by educationists of the inadequacy of education, are all uttered in educational English. Educational English is not at all the same as educated English. It is a curious sort of technical jargon, possibly necessary and suitable to a science or a trade, but casting, as do all such terminologies, a curious air of coldness and unreality upon all that is discussed. It is not the style in which anybody talks; even when it is the style in which somebody unfortunately speaks. It is not the style in which the educationists themselves talk, when they are talking as educated people and not as educationists. This can be felt in the way in which the very words used tend to contradict their own meaning; as in the word, 'individual', in some sweeping generalization about 'giving individual attention'.

It never occurred to the Victorian child, when his nurse

was talking to him in his infancy, that she was giving him 'individual attention'. It might have been quite a large family; but in that sense there were no relations except individual relations. Nor need a nurse of the old sort always consciously individualize; she was quite capable of packing all the children off to bed on the probably sound generalization that the children, as children, were becoming a nuisance. But the point is that the philosophy of the nurse began with one baby and went on to other babies as they arrived. The philosophy of the teacher begins with one class, or one school, and then goes on to decide, with a sigh, that it must give a little more individual attention. The individual is discovered in the mass, as the atom was discovered in the familiar mass that we call matter. But the nurse was nearer to the father and mother, in the fact that the relation was organic and not official. The nurse may have been a mere shadow of the mother; but that sort of shadow is of the same shape. Nay, that sort of shadow is of some substance. Because it is very close to the creative realities of birth and babyhood, it has a quality that can never be described in Educational English. It will never be named at any educational congress. It is difficult enough to name it anywhere; and in most cases it remains nameless because it is natural. And men, especially modern men, are even more afraid of the natural than of the supernatural. But anyhow, if ever we did want to name it, we should never find even a word for it in all those wordy generalizations. It belongs to quite a different sort of English from any Educational English; to that world of words in which men wrote, 'Hast thou not a blessing for me, O my father?'; or, 'The smell of my son is as the smell of a field that the Lord has blessed.' Or in which men said, 'Unto us a Child is born.'

PLAYING WITH AN IDEA

THE serious magazines, without having any convictions to speak of, are just sufficiently stern or bigoted to forbid irreverence. The frivolous magazines are even more stern and bigoted; for they forbid reverence. They actually veto the instinctive mention of mighty and holy things. Thus the sincere journalist is kept constantly in a state of roaring inaction; having been forced to make his theology dry he plunges with a far more boyish ardour into the pleasures of pure folly. But the swing of the pendulum is sometimes rather wild and dizzy. My meaning is this : that a good man ought to love nonsense; but he ought also to see nonsense—that is, to see that it is not sense. Our very pleasure in pure fancies should consist partly in the certainty that they are not facts. Nothing is more perilous and unmanly in modern thought than the way in which people will be led a dance by some dexterous and quite irresponsible suggestion, some theory in which even the theorist does not believe, some intellectual levity which is not honest enough even to be called a lunacy. They hear some flying notion—as that Cromwell wrote Milton, or that Christianity was stolen from the Aztecs; they receive it first laughingly, then fancifully, then speculatively, then seriously, then idolatrously, even to slaying; and yet all the time with nothing to go on but the fourth-hand version of a few entertaining coincidences. Exactly that sort of neat and fantastic solution which would make a glorious detective story is employed to make an utterly preposterous book of history or criticism.

No, I do not think it is wrong to play with these nonsensical hypotheses; I have had great fun out of fitting them together. One of my friends maintains that Tacitus never lived and that his works are a forgery of the sixteenth century; another explains the whole life of St Paul in terms of an unabated hatred for Christianity. I am not against playing the fool with these fancies, but I am against letting them play the fool with me. To take one case at random, one could certainly make a huge theory, upheld by many coincidences, that men's surnames have constantly suited them. It really is a remarkable thing to reflect how many frightfully fine men have had frightfully fine names. How could we have rounded off our sentences without such names as 'Hannibal' and 'Napoleon', or 'Attila' and 'Charlemagne'? But there are more startling cases. There is one great artist whose art was ultimately sacred and seraphic, yet in its labour and technique peculiarly strenuous and military; if one looked at his work only one would think of a harsh angel, an angel in armour. How comes it that this man actually bore the name of the Archangel Michael—Michelangelo? How comes it that a contemporary and more gracious artist happened to be christened after a more gracious archangel —Raphael?

Or take another case. If you or I had to invent out of our own heads a really shattering and shining name, a name fit for some flaming hero defying the stars, a name on horseback and high in the saddle—could we think of any so chivalrous or so challenging as Shakespeare? The very word is like Lancelot at his last tournament with a touch of the divine impotence of Don Quixote. In fact, I know only one surname that is really finer than Shakespeare, and that is Brakespear, the only English Pope. A pleasing lyric in prose might be built up about the two of them; the one Englishman who rose to the highest of all official places, and the other who rose to the highest of all unofficial. Much eloquence and irony (if I had time to write them) might be uttered about the contrast between the English Pope, so humble and silent in his splendid publicity, and the English poet, so hearty and swaggering in his obscurity and neglect. It is at least certain that there was only one Englishman on the highest platform of priests, and only one on the highest platform of poets; and it is certain that each of their names is the only exact rhyme to the other one.

That is what you might call a coincidence; but the coincidence goes further. The actual meaning of the two names is appropriate to the two men in their two positions. If there was one thing more than another that the Renaissance did it was to shake the spear, to brandish the lance even more than to use it, to value the lance more for its flapping pennon than its point. If there was one thing, on the other hand, that a Pope in the twelfth century had to do, it was to break the spear—to bend the thick necks of the throned fighters who could not otherwise have conceived anything so fine as fighting. William Shakespeare is really very like the exultant monster in the Old Testament, who laughs at the shaking of the spear. But Nicholas Brakespear stood in the Dark Ages for a simpler and more searching reminder, of Him who snappeth the spear in twain and takes off the wheel of the chariot.

The above is an impromptu instance of what I call playing with an idea; but the question is, what does one think of the idea? I will tell you what I think of it; I think it is complete bosh. I am almost certain that Raphael and Michelangelo are a coincidence. I am almost certain that Shakespeare and Brakespear are an accidental rhyme. I will carry the fancy as far as I choose; but if it tries to carry me as far as it chooses, I will remind it of several things. I will point out to it that in plain fact the names of literary men are often quite arrestingly unsuitable. Newman was by no means a worshipper of novelty; and one of the most energetic and intelligent atheists of my acquaintance is saddled with the surname of Priest.

Or take a classic example. Can anyone read the cold and cutting work of Swift without feeling that his surname should have been Steele? Can anyone read the impetuous work of Steele without feeling that his surname should have been Swift? We should really feel much happier if we could talk of the brilliant blunders of Dick Swift and the cool, saturnine strength of Jonathan Steele. In other words, my speculation about surnames is just large enough to fill a magazine article, but is not large enough to fill even a moderate-sized brain. It is this power of recovery after extravagance that I urgently recommend. Indulge in all the most decadent or futile fantasies, as long as you can curb the indulgence, like that of alcohol. Ride on the nightmare, if you prefer such horseflesh; only do not let the nightmare ride on you. Find the mare's nest which rocks on the tallest and darkest trees, and steal the addled eggs; but do not make your breakfast off them every morning for ever. Learn to be nonsensical and then to be sensible again; to create strange things and still to be independent of them. Learn to suggest a thing, to urge it, to prove it, and still to disbelieve it. For the very few things that are really worth believing are not worth proving.

THE WALKING PARADOX

THE English People have a peculiar appetite for paradox. I suppose such a statement will itself be called a paradox; for the phrase is commonly applied, for some reason or other, not to Englishmen generally, but to the one sad and solitary Englishman who bears alone, in this column, the doom or judgement upon his race. Both he and his race, however, remain reasonably cheerful under it; and, though it is rather a bore to be called paradoxical, it is rather a compliment to be recognized as national. Nevertheless, there are shades of variety, and the mad Englishman may wear his wild rose with a difference. The curious thing about the representative Englishman of the last few centuries is that he instinctively pursued the wildest paradox and then accepted it as a solid truism. He said he was hard-headed, and stood on his head to prove it.

For instance, saying, 'We may not understand political theories, but our constitution works well in practice', is a piece of wild paradox and only loved as such, like a nonsense rhyme of Lear or Lewis Carroll. It is exactly like saying, 'We cannot add up figures correctly; we are quite content if the result comes out right.' It is like saying, 'It is true that we got the wrong longitude and the wrong latitude; but what does that matter when it means that we find the place we are looking for?' There is no answer to this beautiful nonsense, except to say that we do not get the right result or find the right place, except in the Great Gromboolian Plain or the Land Where the Jumblies Live. But it is a beautiful land to live in, and it is remarkably like England. Of course, anything in England that was really practical was achieved in spite of neglecting the theoretical, and not because of it. But anything in England that was poetical, as distinct from practical, really did owe something to this taste for paradox. In this sense the other name of England is Elfland. From this spirit comes all that quaintness in the names of places or in the very plan of towns which is so delightful a feature of England and which is now being steadily destroyed.

Even in the nonsense rhymes to which I have referred, there is a constant unconscious groping after this native tradition. Not for nothing did even the nonsense rhymer bear a name out of ancient British legend and literature; so that the merry madman was a sort of parody of the melancholy madman. One might almost write another grim and grotesque scene of madness, of the meeting between the tragic Lear and the comic Lear. But both are full of that quality of quaintness; that quality that prevents the tragic hero, even when he is most tragic, from being entirely heroic; or, at any rate, from being entirely classic. The height from which a man in King Lear looks dizzily down is not a mountain or a Tower of Babel, but only one of those chalk cliffs that are to us the white walls of home. And when the nonsense rhymer invents a nonsense place and calls it The Chankley Bore, we feel by the very sound of it that it might be in Sussex.

Or, again, there is nothing but paradox in the whole legend of the Strong Silent Man, as in the legend of the Dong with the Luminous Nose. Indeed, I remember suggesting that historical students may some day explain the inexplicable lyric by calling it a contemporary satire on Oliver Cromwell, who was jeered at in his own time for having a red nose, and revered in our time, far less reasonably, for being a Strong Silent Man. As a matter of fact, he may have been strong, but he was the very reverse of silent. He talked a great deal; and that is one of the things that makes me think there was really something in him. But anyhow, it is nonsense to assume that a man must have something in him merely because you cannot get anything out of him. It is a pure paradox itself. The natural and sensible assumption would be that a man who has anything to say will want to say it. And, nine times out of ten, anybody who really has anything to say does want to say it. He would be rather an unpleasant fellow if he did not. Indeed, he would be not much more reputable than a miser. It is no more admirable to have valuable suggestions to make and not put them into circulation than it is to have valuable coin of the realm and keep it stuffed into a greasy old stocking.

Of course it is quite true that various accidents or conditions may keep a worthy man silent when he really is in the right; such as his being shy, his being born deaf and dumb, his being gagged by burglars and left alone in the coal-cellar, his being entrusted with a secret, or his being afflicted with a stammer. But these are exceptions. There may be strong silent men, as there may be strong deaf men, or strong short-sighted men. But deafness does not strengthen anybody; nor does strength in itself obscure the eyesight. The truth is that the whole of this notion is, if not entirely nonsensical, at least entirely poetical. The fancy fascinates the English temper, because there is in it a purely romantic effect of transition and surprise. It is obvious that it makes a better story, and especially a better play, if the quiet man in the corner suddenly takes the centre of the stage and reveals the secret of the drama. It is not unnatural that the nation which produced the greatest of dramatists should have a taste for such effects of drama.

What is curious about the English psychology is this; that it has this purely artistic appetite and then persuades itself that it is practical. The notion of the vainglorious person, with his heart on his sleeve, defeated by the strong man, who has something more valuable up his sleeve, is a story that had been the foundation of a hundred farces and fanciful comedies and romantic melodramas before it was made the basis of a scientific theory of races or a scheme of the British Constitution. The strong silent gentleman had been in all sorts of shoddy or shabby theatrical parts; he had been the good brother and the bad baronet and the stranger and the first walking gentleman, and even Charles's Friend, before it was discovered by science that he was the Nordic man and the sane and practical Anglo-Saxon.

In other words, we have as a nation got our ideas out of novels and plays and poetical romances, much more than out of economic textbooks or even commercial ledgers. That sort of fiction is naturally full of paradox; or, in other words, full of surprise. It is the whole point of a fairy-tale to say that the fool found a windfall of amazing good fortune. Therefore we said that a politician who did not think about politics would somehow or other muddle through. It is the whole point of a melodrama that the man whose lips have been sealed until the last moment comes forward and declares the innocence of the heroine or the hiding-place of the will. Therefore we said that any politician who was incompetent to speak must always be competent to act.

All this belongs to a world of wild and yet subtle inversion with which I can sympathize; which, in its proper place, I am even prepared to defend. But practical politics is not its proper place; and our politics have not been more practical for following only this flying gleam of paradox. In this matter we really do need a little more of the iron common sense of the Latins, who know that schemes and systems are made with logic, just as machines and engines are made with mathematics. Just as they know that two and two make four, so they know that thinking is really necessary to acting. There is really something to be said for platitudes and plain intellectual processes; and the French peasant has remained very invincible in his own kitchen garden by dint of knowing how many beans make five. But it takes all sorts to make a world; and France has not produced Shakespeare or a nonsense rhyme.

THE COLOUR OF SPAIN

IT is to be hoped that people will realize that Spain is not so black as it was painted by those who only painted the black hoods of the Inquisitors or the Tennysonian dualism of Don and Devil. Spain in one sense is quite as black as it is painted, for the painters were particularly fond of painting in black. But being in black is by no means the same as being in mourning. We might almost say that the Spaniards are fond of bright colours and that black is the brightest of all their colours. They are very fond of it in art and decoration but the effect is not necessarily what the English used to call gloomy but rather what the French have called *chic*. It throws up all the other colours, especially the typically Spanish colours of gold and orange and copper and dark red. There are aspects in which all Spain seems to be striped with red and gold like the legendary shield of Aragon. But nothing could make that glowing shield glow more vividly than to be worn by a knight in black armour or carried by a page in black velvet.

The well-known picture of the Spanish lady wearing a black mantilla and a red rose would be sufficient to make us recognize the tradition. The mantilla alone shows that black is a gay colour and almost the colour of frivolity. For the Spanish ladies who keep the old custom in this respect look far more like what the old ballads call 'ladies gay', the dames of a joyous Court, or the dancing girls of a jovial festival, than do the more modernized ladies who have obediently hidden their heads in the helmets of the last Parisian fashion. The colour of the Spanish scarf or veil is dark, but it is not dismal; it is bright because it is brisk; it can shift and change with posture and gesture and mood; it is alive like a black snake or a black bird or a black butterfly. The accident that some of Velasquez's great portraits have a sombre dignity that is almost Satanic, and that Goya made black-and-white studies that are like the sketch-book of a goblin, should not lead us to exaggerate the sombre side of this use of black. The Spaniards do indeed use it where nobody else I know of has ever used it. I have actually seen black patches in a coloured church window. This is contrary to the very conception of windows, but it is quite consistent with the Spanish conception of colours.

The same impression, and perhaps the same illusion, is doubtless produced by the Spanish churches which are kept unusually and to us unnaturally dark. It would seem as if the architect, like the artist, wished to produce great blocks of black and did it with great blocks of shadow. The altars and the altar-screens are prodigiously high and heavy like the portals of the palaces of giants. They seem to make the darkness darker, throwing a shadow even upon shade. Yet even here we find the triumph of contrast which is really the triumph of colour. The stained-glass windows are turned to swords of flame of an indescribable incandescence. The church is dark with the very density of its colour. The Spanish gold may be partly buried in the gloom, just as the Spanish gold of romance was so often buried in the green sea. But in the reality, as in the romance, we always think of the treasure as tremendously costly and complex and covering vast areas. Indeed, there is sometimes a sensation in these twilight churches of walking as if in the depths of the sea; as if the hundreds of little candles were a phosphorescence or

C

the great canopies and banners the shapes of flat and floating fishes of gigantic size.

The contrast struck me very sharply when I had crossed the Pyrenees, and found again the French spirit in the church and castle of Carcassonne, in an open lantern of lofty windows luminous as the soul of St Louis. But though the French spirit has more clarity it has not more colour; it has not really more gaiety. There are all sorts of gaiety even in the Spanish churches, when once we understand them; there is any amount of it in the Spanish streets and houses. There is all that spirit that is so puzzling to many people in the religious processions associated with Seville. I say associated with Seville be-cause, as a matter of fact, the association is much too arbitrary and limited. Most people imagine that the fantastic dance of dwarfs and giants is something that can be seen only at Seville, as the Eiffel Tower can be seen only in Paris. I, for one, did not even go to Seville but I saw, and heard any amount about, such dances and processions in any number of other towns and villages. These ancient games and gaieties have been preserved in the past all over the Spanish peninsula; yet I fear that there are very few tourists who trouble much about them in their less famous habitations. They are few indeed compared with the number of tourists who deliberately rush to see bull-fights in order to boast that they cannot bear the sight.

I may remark, in passing, that I did not go to see any bull-fights, for a reason which I explained to my Spanish friends on the spot. I said I should be very much annoyed if one of my Spanish friends came to England and in-stantly put on pink that he might rush to the meet and be in at the death of a poor little fox and then turn round and say, 'How hideous! How repulsive! What brutes in human form are the English whose whole lives are passed in this degrading sport!' We can indulge in all sorts of controversy and casuistry about bull-fighting or fox-hunting and there is a great deal to be said against both. All countries have anomalies that strike us as abnormalities or even abominations; but it is not seeing a country to look for the things that you abominate. Now I know that the Spaniards I saw are a kind people; they are astonishingly kind to children; they are not normally unkind to animals. There is a home for stray cats actually kept in the cloisters of the cathedral of Tarragona; and I have seen crowds of cats gathered round the image of St Ramon Nonato like the crowds of birds round St Francis. There are plenty of ordinary people making friends with dogs and horses in the ordinary way. But if I had preferred a Grand Guignol thrill to a great experience of a great nation, I might have allowed it to get between me and all these things.

But this is a parenthesis; I was remarking that the celebrated procession at Seville is only the special and supreme example of a custom that is scattered all over these southern lands. The way in which religious mysteries are mixed with merry-making is very shocking to some people—especially, I have noticed, to the people who do not believe in the religious mysteries. Sceptics are so very sensitive on the point of reverence. But as I came in contact with these things, I could not but smile at the thought of those who have again been trying to prove to me that religion has no function but to make men sad. Those who gradually built up the ancient customs of mankind had a better sense of proportion and decoration. They knew, if only by instinct, how things grave and gay can be combined and distributed and where flippancy is fitting and where solemnity fits in with it; what contrast will best bring out a real severity and what is the psychological meaning of that profound phrase 'comic relief'; just as the people of that southern land have always known, in dress and decoration, how a great blot of black brings out their crimson and their gold.

THE TRADITION OF TOLEDO

ONE of the first impressions created by a visit to Spain, in any person with any historical imagination, is the sense of a world that runs round the Mediterranean rather than of three separate worlds which the sea divides. It is, I suppose, what the old world meant by talking of the round or circle of the lands. The point is that a man might sail from port to port round the whole of that inland sea and find something at least linking all those places together. If he pierced further into the various continents he would doubtless find things very different: very different if he plunged into what we call the African forests; very different if he set out on what we call the Asiatic plains. But a great deal that we imagine to be Asiatic in Lebanon, or African in Algiers, is really of the mixed central civilization, and at least as much European as the more Moorish parts of Spain. I think it is because people see this when they are not expecting it that they can make nothing of it and their descriptions are so unconvincing and conventional. For when people see what they do not understand they do not even believe what they see.

Thus Toledo looked to me much more like Jerusalem than Jerusalem ever looked like most of the pictures of it. It has a wall crowning a hill whose steep sides have an indefinable look of a ruin and even a rubbish-heap. It is in the sort of country that is spotted with hardy olives or striped with hardy vines. It has that look that we never know in the rich rain and deep grasses of our northern islands—the look of vegetation being an exception. It is a green object and not merely a green background. For we owe our green fields to our grey clouds; and perhaps do not thank them often enough for it. In those splendid Spanish ruins a man feels immediately that he is within a circle or radius of something that lay to the south, and that the same radius also touched Jerusalem at the ends of the earth.

It is not easy to define what that circle is. Those unduly discontented with the grey clouds may be inclined to say that it is simply the circle of the sun. But I am inclined to think it is also the circle of a culture and a historical tradition, which touches all these places though it varies from place to place. There is something in common between those opposite ends of the earth, or at least of the sea. The Crusaders have been in Jerusalem; the Moors have been in Toledo. But the conventional conception that cut up the world into four quarters in the old style does not look for such a similarity. It does not expect it; it cannot be expected to expect it. It expects Jerusalem to be only an Asiatic bazaar like Baghdad or even Bombay. It expects Toledo to be concentrated on Toledo swords like Sheffield on Sheffield cutlery. In many ways Toledo is very like a sword, steely and of a stern sort of chivalry; but it is warmed from the south; it is in the circle of the sun.

I know it is customary to talk about the Moorish influence, as if what is really the Mediterranean influence was always a Moslem influence. This I believe to be a complete mistake. The indefinable connexion that links a town like Toledo to a town like Jerusalem existed long before Mahomet was born. It remained essentially a Christian connexion long after Mahomet's religion had first swept over these places and at last retreated from them. We may call it, if we like, the Roman influence, though even that is insufficient. We may connect it with our own view of the Christian unity, though that will naturally be a matter of dispute. But whatever it is, it did not come out of the desert with the dry negations of a desert creed. It did not plant all those vineyards with the veto of Islam upon wine. It did not carve all those images with the veto of Islam upon statues. It did not find the chivalric devotion to the lady by looking for it in the harem, or all the legends of the Mother and the Holy Child from the arid Arabian dogma of the isolation of God.

The tradition for which Toledo still lifts its riven crown of roofs and battlements may have been stirred to life by movements out in the East, or mingled to advantage with strange and remote things; it may have gained as well as given something in its contact with the Arab conquerors of Africa; but it is certain, if anything is certain, that when that spirit of Spain and of Western Christianity was touched to new life, it was in the form of its own life that it unfolded and to the height of its own destiny that it rose again; and Islam did not make a new world in such places, but only awakened a world that was asleep. That world is now very wide awake; and if the cathedral of Toledo was not merely modelled on a mosque even when the world was swept by the Moslem, it is now even less likely that featureless mosques will be the only churches of the future.

TOM JONES AND THE ESCORIAL

I wonder how many people have noticed that a famous quotation from Gibbon can now be classed with the fulfilled prophecies—or rather, what is even more mystic and oracular, with the half-fulfilled prophecies. I say a quotation from Gibbon, for I fear it would be more misleading to call it a passage in Gibbon. Gibbon is now a classic; that is, he is quoted instead of being read. The thing most commonly quoted is an unusually stark and startling lie; the story which identifies St George with an Arian who was a swindling contractor. It is still sometimes quoted as a truth; though it is hard to understand how anybody with even the most superficial sense of history could ever have thought it true. Supposing, for the sake of argument, that the Church had been enthusiastically eager to canonize a swindler, it would have been quite impossible for her to canonize a heretic. But more often nowadays it is quoted as a lie; for the historian's cold hatred of the Christian tradition has begun to be felt and allowed for; but, as it is one of the few things quoted at all, it might be held to imply that the whole history was a tissue of lies. And this would be quite as unjust to Gibbon as Gibbon was to George. But there has been a reaction against that Age of Reason, in which we may lose even those parts of it that were really reasonable. Whatever else we may say of our own age, for good or evil, nobody is likely to call it an Age of Reason. The later French Pantheists called Voltaire a barbarian, exactly as Voltaire had called Shakespeare a barbarian. And in the same way even the 'Decline and Fall' has already declined and fallen.

But there is one other quotation from it that still deserves to be called a popular quotation. Being a popular quotation, it is probably a popular misquotation. Such a thing is normally misquoted; and I will here, to the best of my humble ability, misquote it. I have not got the book within reach; and I would not be bothered to look through the whole six volumes even if I had. But it is a passage in which he remarks, in a sort of parenthesis, that the family of Henry Fielding was connected in some way with the Imperial House of the Holy Roman Empire; and admits that the great princes of the dynasty might smile at the connexion; 'but the romance of Tom Jones, that exquisite picture of life and manners, will outlive the palace of the Escorial and the imperial eagle of Austria'.

Well, it has already outlived the imperial eagle of Austria. That half of the defiant prediction has already become a definite and rather dull fact; almost in the way of an anti-climax. And it could not but cross my mind, like a cloud of some strange shape crossing the sky, when I stood recently under the ranked and rigid columns of the Escorial, that strange Spanish palace built by the harsh whim of one of the strangest of Spaniards and of men. Philip the Second not only dedicated it to St Laurence, but built it in the shape of a gridiron. And I realized something appropriate in the image, beyond the suggestion of something in the King's own life of stiffness and of suffering. Señor Junoy, the distinguished Catalan writer, said to me, with great imaginative insight : 'It seems so cold, and yet it is so ardent.' Philip's gridiron, almost like Pickwick's warming-pan, was a cover for hidden fire. The very coldness of the surroundings accentuates that contained intensity.

Others besides myself have often remarked on the curious fact that the guide-books and note-books of travel,

and all the countless sketches and photographs and similar
records, never seem to tell us the thing which seems most
striking when it strikes the eye. I had heard about Philip
the Second and the Escorial, and other elements in the
picture; but I conceived a picture of Spain rather as if it
must be a picture of Seville. I thought vaguely that everything would happen in the summer and there would be
a background of orange-trees and a hint of Moorish architecture. I had seen hundreds and hundreds of sketches
and pictures of Spanish scenes, often probably of these
identical Spanish scenes; and yet somehow the primary
point of the whole impression had never pierced.

Nobody had ever told me—at least, nobody had ever
told me so that I realized and remembered it—that the
Spanish King had done something altogether unique and
even unnatural when he built in such a place and in such
a style his grim gridiron of stone. Nobody had made me
understand that he had built a palace almost on the top
of a mountain, far away upon naked and sterile heights
only approached by rocky and ruinous roads like mountain passes. He had built a palace where anyone else
would have built a hermitage. Like a madman, he had
reared his tower of pomp and pride in a howling wilderness, where he might literally hear the wolves howl.

Yet there was nothing extravagant or fantastic in his
architectural achievement; it was too sternly classical to
be classed even with the Baroque. It is said that he sat
outside watching it being built, with the plans in his hand
and his gouty foot on a stool; jealously vigilant to see that
not a curve of too much exuberance should soften that
terrible triangle. A curious and not very pleasant person
though genuine in his way; but he did great harm in one
respect. He was a Puritan on the wrong side; that is, he
was on what I should call the right side, but it was not the

side of the Puritans. He was very unlike most Spaniards but he has come to stand as a type of all of them. And under the shadow of his mere individuality we forget the real light and shade in the whole picture. We forget that his religious enemies were mostly Calvinists and men even more gloomy than he, and gloomy on principle as well as by accident. In his unlucky version of the legend of St Laurence, he was himself so much more like a persecutor than a martyr that he made any martyr look like a saint. We forget that most of the martyrs were Calvinists, who would have built something much more inhuman than the Escorial, only they were too inhuman to build anything at all. Perhaps he also forgot that, in the original legend, St Laurence joked on the gridiron.

I think the prophecy of Gibbon, like the prayer of somebody in Virgil, will be half fulfilled and half scattered to the winds. I do not anticipate the decline and fall of the Escorial; I think it would take a good deal to remove that formidable object, a good deal more than is needed for the rather artificial revolution that altered an Austrian postage stamp. For Spain is fortunate in having had her decline and fall, and being now (I think) quite clearly rising once more. The Escorial has survived the fall, and there seems no reason why it should fall with the resurrection. But I do certainly hope that in another sense its shadow may grow a little less, as has the shadow of the imperial eagle. For a long time past the Escorial had stood for Philip the Second and Philip the Second had stood for Spain. Whatever is harsh or sombre in this one particular palace of this one particular prince has been associated with a whole people, who are not, in fact, in the least harsh or sombre, but in many ways exceedingly genial and generous. He was not at all a typical Spaniard, any more than Louis XI was a typical Frenchman, or Henry

VII a typical Englishman—or even Welshman. But the imperial eagle has come to seem a bird of ill omen, and his castle a ruin fit for the nesting of such fowls of night. I certainly hope that, as an international impression, that error will pass away, and that Gibbon's prophecy may yet serve to remind us that Spain is the home of the picaresque romance, or rambling comedy, and is not as gloomy as the Escorial, but as jolly as Tom Jones.

POETRY IN ACTION

IF I were asked why I think our whole industrial society is cursed with sterility and stamped with the mark of the slave, I could give a great many answers, but one will serve for the moment: because it cannot create a custom. It can only create a fashion. Now a fashion is simply something that has failed to be a custom. It is changed as a fashion because it is a failure as a custom. The rich, who are the most restless of mankind, do one thing after another and prove in the very process that they cannot create anything that is good enough to last. Their succession of fashions is in itself a succession of failures. For when men have made really dignified and humane things they have always desired that they should remain or, at least, that some relic of them should remain.

We have statues of all schools of statuary and buildings of all periods of architecture. But fashion, in the feverish sense that exists today, is a totally different thing, a merely destructive thing; indeed, an entirely negative thing. It is as if a man were perpetually carving a statue and smashing it as soon as he carved it; as if he were always clumsily fumbling with the clay and had never modelled it to his liking. It is as if people began to dig up the foundations of a house before they had finished putting the roof on. This is not activity or energy or efficiency; it is certainly not efficiency, for it never achieves its effect; it never regards it as either effective or effectual. It is simply instability and discontent; and one of the marks of it is that it cannot create a custom. It cannot, for instance, create a ceremonial, still less a legend. It can sometimes attempt a rag or a practical joke; it can attempt that very dismal sort of dinner that the millionaires in America call a Freak. But the thing cannot be repeated; even the stupidest millionaire could not stand that.

When the traveller visits a place like Spain, the first thing that strikes him is a change from this atmosphere of hard and barren frivolity to the atmosphere of grave and solemn festivity. The Spaniards still have customs rather than fashions; and their customs come natural to them. They do not need to be changed, because to fresher minds they are always fresh. This is particularly true, for instance, about the sort of ceremonial that everywhere gathers round childhood. In such places it is not only children who understand childhood. Grown-up people understand it so thoroughly that they themselves become what the wise call childlike and the foolish call childish. It can be seen in a hundred things that make a system of communication between two generations. But it can be seen in this above all; that the grown-up people are still capable of inventing a ceremony, as children invent a game. The ceremonies vary, not only from place to place, but from century to century. They are not all old, as antiquaries like things to be old; for antiquaries only like things to be antiquated. Just as these living peasantries renew their fields and farms, so they renew their habitations and habits. Just as they restore their churches, by putting new patches on to old buildings, so they renew their games and jokes, putting in many elements in one place which are not found in another.

What is called the Seville procession exists in many different places besides Seville. But as it is done in many different places, so it is done in many different ways. There are often elements that are in their nature new, that are unexpected in the sense that nobody could possibly expect them. I have heard it said that, sometimes, a man will rush out into the path of the procession and pour out a stream of absurdly spontaneous poetry, like an improvisation on a musical instrument; and that sometimes somebody else (also rather abruptly moved by the Muse) will answer him from a window with appropriate poetical repartees. But the point is that the old framework allows of these new things, just as the old orchard bears fresh fruit or the old garden fresh flowers. These old civilizations give us the sensation of being always at the beginning of things; whereas mere modern innovation gives us the sensation, even in its novelty, of drawing nearer and nearer to the end.

There is one custom in Spain, and probably in other southern countries, which might be a model of the popular instinct for poetry in action. It is what corresponds to our idea of Santa Claus, who is, of course, St Nicolas, and in the North the patron of children and the giver of gifts at Christmas. In the South this function is performed by the Three Kings, and the gifts are given at the Epiphany. It is in a sense more logical, which, perhaps, is why is is common among the Latins. The Wise Men are in any case bringing gifts to the Holy Child, and they bring them at the same time to the human children. But there is in connexion with it an excellent example of how people who retain this popular instinct can actually act a poem.

The mysterious Kings arrive at the end of the holiday, which again is really very reasonable. It is much better that the games and dances and dramas, which are fugitive, should come first and the children be left with the presents, or permanent possessions, at the end. But it is also the occasion of a process very mystical and moving to the imagination. The Kings are conceived as coming nearer and nearer every day; and, if there are images of these sacred figures, they are moved from place to place every night. That alone is strangely thrilling, either considered as a child's game or as a mystic's meditation on the mysteries of time and space. On the last night of all, when the strange travellers through time are supposed to arrive, the children carefully put out water and green stuff for the camels and the horses of that superhuman cavalcade out of the depths of the East. Even the touch of putting water, so necessary to purely Eastern animals, is enough to suggest that reach of the imagination to the ends of the earth.

Now, that is only one example, out of hundreds that can be collected in any valley or countryside, of something which people in simpler times had the power to create; a complete and concrete drama perfectly plain and unfathomably profound. What I want to know about modern civilization, which in many ways cares so much for beauty, which in some ways cares far too much for beauty, is why it cannot produce these beautiful things. I do not want it to copy Spain and the Three Kings, or to copy Scandinavia and St Nicolas, or to copy any particular local ritual. But why can it never invent anything of its own? I have long paused for a reply.

THE ROMANCE OF HISTORY

THE signs of the resurrection of Spain of which I think there are many to be seen lately, have turned my thoughts to certain subtleties in the tradition of that land. They are things so subtle that they always appear to be simple. One of them is the tradition of chivalry and the double attitude towards it which we connect with the name of Don Quixote. There is no more fantastic paradox in all history than the life and work of Cervantes. He is generally recognized as having written a book to show that romantic adventures are all rubbish and do not really happen in this world. As a matter of fact, the one man in this world to whom romantic adventures were incessantly happening was the author of 'Don Quixote'. He covered himself with glory and lost his right hand at the most romantic battle in history—when the Crescent and the Cross met in the blue Mediterranean by the Isles of Greece, trailing all their pageants of painted and gilded ships with emblazoned sails. He was just about to receive public recognition from the victor, Don John of Austria, when he was kidnapped by pirates. He organized a series of escapes, each like the ideal adventure of a schoolboy; he organized supplies and comforts for his fellow-prisoners with the laborious altruism of a saint. As men go, he was really a pretty perfect pattern of the knight of chivalry; eventually he escaped and returned home to write a book showing that chivalry was impossible. At least, that is what three rationalistic centuries have taken it as showing. But I think the time has come to dig a little deeper in that

D   39

stratified irony and show the other side of Cervantes and chivalry.

Hero-worship has fallen out of fashion with Carlyle, who forced it into fashion. But in the case of Carlyle there were circumstances that were a needless handicap of hero-worship and even to heroism. Carlyle set himself the impossible task of making heroes out of the successful men of history and politics. It was not much more hopeful than that of making heroes out of the successful men in soap or petrol. In one sense that sort of hero-worship is heroic, in the sense of being impossible. The task is heroic because the subject is unheroic. In Carlyle's characteristic work it soon ran into absurdity. It reached the point of praising Frederick the Great—a form of hero-worship which is clearly a *reductio ad absurdum*, and even almost a contradiction in terms. The character of Cromwell had more human elements; but what was best in it was human and emphatically not heroic. The best case for Cromwell is that he was a moderately sane man in a very insane age. His best work was done as a moderator and maker of compromises, not as an originator or inspirer of enthusiasms. He saved works of art which the wilder Puritans would have destroyed, but we cannot picture him as a great patron of art in the sense of a friend of artists. He insisted that there must be good pay for good soldiers; but he was not the sort of man to be a romance to his own soldiers, like Napoleon. He was a seventeenth-century English squire whose family had grown rich in the great pillage; and morally he was no worse than most of his kind and perhaps better than many of them. He was certainly much better than Frederick the Great whom Carlyle made even more of a hero, and even a god.

The worship of Frederick the Great can hardly be called hero-worship. It is rather devil-worship softened by a touch of monkey-worship. It is superstitution and therefore heresy to say such things seriously, but we may say symbolically that if a demon could enter the body of a monkey the result might be something like Frederick II of Prussia. It is not only true that he had a large mind and a small soul, it might almost equally truly be said that he had a large brain and a small mind. Even his intellectual pride was petty. Moreover, he was in another sense curiously like a monkey. He was an imitator. As the old mystics used to say that the devil was the ape of God, we might more literally say that Frederick II was the ape of Louis XIV. But just as the monkey imitates the man without understanding the man, just as the ape can copy an action that he cannot comprehend, so the Prussian had nothing of the national and civilized quality of the Frenchman. He substituted a new impudence and malignity for the last trailing tradition of medieval chivalry and Roman law. But Carlyle had to make a hero out of him, on his own theory of the heroism of success. Frederick had nothing else except success—not even the power to enjoy it.

But when we have got rid of this sort of hero-worship we may really come back to heroes. There really were heroes who were historical characters though they were not generally successful men. More often the true hero was a tragic hero. But while his tale was often a tragedy in so far as he failed, it was often a wildly impossible romance in the moments when he triumphed. The curious thing is that real history is much more romantic, and not less romantic, than Carlyle made it out. The hero may sometimes have lost his campaign, but he won his battles. And he can often be seen winning his battles single-handed like the most legendary knight winning his spurs. Chivalry really did succeed in doing the impracticable things, even when it failed to do the practical things. We may differ or feel doubtful about the ultimate success or even the ultimate value of various policies pursued in the past; but nobody can doubt the thrill and enthusiasm and courage of the pursuit. The only really reliable part of history is the romance of it.

For instance, Godfrey de Bouillon died young, wasted by a fever that might have been cured in more sanitary conditions and wearied with a problem which was perhaps almost insoluble. That is a tragedy of the modern sort; it may well be said that his life was a failure; it might be said that the Crusades were a failure. We might argue about whether he was a maker, a builder, a man who can, or any of the Carlylean descriptions. For those depend on elaborate historical results which arise later; and the end of everything arrives sooner or later. It is disputable whether Richelieu was a successful man, since the French monarchy went down in the French Revolution. It is disputable whether Frederick the Great was a successful man, since Prussianized Germany went down in the Great War. So it is disputable whether Godfrey was a successful man, since the Latin Kingdom of Jerusalem went down in the disaster of Hattin. What is quite indisputable is that Godfrey was a hero of romance, a hero of the wildest and most improbable romance, a hero behaving as heroes behave in the extravagant romances of chivalry. What is certain is that he, the Commander-in-Chief of the whole military system of Europe in the East, did really behave in the manner of Dick Dauntless among the Redskins or How a Powder-Monkey Foiled the Pirates. It is a cold and concrete fact that he was himself the first to leap from the battle-tower on to the Saracenic turrets, exactly as the boy who ran away to sea is the first to leap from his battle-ship on to the slaver's deck. All that part of the business that was a statesman's calculation may or may not have been falsified. All that part of it that was like a schoolboy's daydream came true.

There are any number of other examples of the kind. Nelson is too near to us for us to be certain of the duration of his practical achievement; but the nearer we are to him the less doubt we have of his purely poetical achievement. Near as he is to us, he is nearer still to the morning of the world, and has the colour and the clear outline that belongs to the primitive legends of the dawn. We do not know how long the naval leadership of England will last, but we do know that the legend will last. We do not know how far aviation has altered everything or how far politicians would go in the direction of scrapping the British Navy. But we do know that Nelson could hardly have been a more mythical figure if he had flown upon wings; or that his ship might have been a fairy-ship and hardly shone more strangely on the storied sea. The things that are quite certain about Nelson are all the improbable things; that he died in the very hour of triumph; that he died on a vessel that bore the very name of victory; that he was shot through wearing the flaming stars with which he had just offered to die in honour—all the coincidences that would be called crude and far-fetched in a story. They are the fancies that are considered a little too romantic for historical fiction. They are also the only fixed facts of history.

THE HERALDIC LION

SIR THOMAS BROWNE was, as everybody knows, a medical man. He was a rather curious kind of medical man; and there are a great many points in which he presents a somewhat singular contrast to our doctors of today. For instance, he wrote an eloquent and exhaustive work on urn-burial, churchyards, and death generally; a subject which doctors are now understood to avoid. But in nothing is he so permanently interesting as in his relations with the remarkable zoology of his time. His superb religious rhetoric and the whole literary side of him are obviously immortal. Nothing finer has ever been said about the soul than that phrase of Browne's that it is a thing in man 'which owes no homage unto the sun'. But a more delicate defence is needed of his quaint science, and, indeed, of all the medieval science from which he drew his ideas. We know that his theology was true. We know that his zoology was untrue; but do not let us too readily assume that it is therefore unimportant. The whole of that old, fantastic science is misunderstood. It made every creature rather a symbol than a fact. But, then, it thought that all material facts were valuable as symbols of spiritual facts. It did not really very much mind whether the lion was a noble animal who spared virgins. What it did want to make clear was that, if the lion was a noble animal, it would spare virgins.

Let me take this example of what I mean. Every modern person of intelligence can see quite easily that the heraldic lion is very different from the real lion. But what we moderns do not quite realize is this: that the heraldic lion is much more important than the real lion. Words positively fail me to express the unimportance of the real lion. The real lion is a large, hairy sort of cat that happens to be living (or rather happens to be dying) in useless deserts that we have never seen and never want to see; a creature that never did us any good, and, in our circumstances, cannot even do us any harm; a thing as trivial, for all our purposes, as the darkest of the deep-sea fishes or as the minerals in the moon. There is no earthly reason to suppose that he has any of the leonine qualities as we ordinarily understand them. There is no ground for imagining that he is generous or heroic, or even proud. Some people who have fought him say that he is not even brave. He does not touch human life at any point at all. You cannot turn him, as you can the ox, into a labourer : nor can you turn him, as you can the dog, into a sportsman and a gentleman. He can share neither our toils nor our pleasures : you cannot harness a lion to a plough, nor can you, with a pack of lions, go hunting an elephant. He has no human interest about him. He is not even good to eat. From the fringe of his mangy and overrated mane to the tip of his tail (with which, I understand, he hits himself in order to overcome the natural cowardice of his disposition), from his mane to his tail, I say, he is one mass of unimportance. He is simply an overgrown stray cat. And he is a stray cat that never comes into our street. He is living his commonplace existence in regions where no white man can live without going mad with monotony and heat. We have to put him in our museums and such places, just as we have to put tiny little chips of grey stone that look as if you could pick them up in the street, or homely-looking brown beetles at which no self-respecting child could look twice.

But the only kind of lion that is of any earthly practical

importance is the legendary lion. He really is a useful thing to have about the place. He holds up the shield of England, which would otherwise fall down, despite the well-meant efforts of the Unicorn, whose hoofs are deficient in a prehensile quality. The African lion does not matter to anyone. But the British Lion, though he does not exist, does matter. He means something; it is the only true object of existence to mean something; and the real African lion has never succeeded in meaning anything at all. The legendary lion, the lion that was made by man and not by Nature, he is indeed the king of beasts. He is a great work of art, a great creation of the genius of man, like Rouen Cathedral or the Iliad. We know his character perfectly well, as we know the character of Mr Micawber, or many other persons who have never taken the trouble to exist in a mere material way. His virtues are the virtues of a grand European gentleman; there is nothing African about his ethics. He has the sense of the sanctity and dignity of death which is behind so many of our ancient rites. He will not touch the dead. He has that strange worship of a bright and proud chastity which is the soul of our Europe, in Diana, in the Virgin Martyrs, in Britomart, which left a single white star in the sensual storms of the Elizabethan Drama, and which is reconquering the world in its new form—the worship of children. The lion will not hurt virgins. In an innumerable number of the old legends and poems you will find the description of the refusal of some eminent lion to touch some eminent young lady. Some say that this sense of delicacy is mutual; and that young ladies also refuse to touch lions. This may be true : but even if it is true it probably only applies to the lower or actual lion, the mere lion of Africa, a negligible creature whom we have already dismissed to wander in his deserts, deserts which are as futile as himself and which form the dustbin of the universe. The valuable lion, we have agreed, is a creature made entirely by man, like the chimaera and the hippogriff, the mermaid and the centaur, the giant with a hundred eyes, and the giant with a hundred hands. The lion on one side of the royal shield is as fabulous as the unicorn on the other side. In so far as he is not merely fantastic and impossible, he consists of all the aggregate good qualities of a kind of super-celestial country gentleman. The heraldic lion is fading, I fear, upon our escutcheons. He still swings valiantly, however, over certain places of entertainment where so many of the kindlier traditions of our ancient civilization have taken refuge. If you see the Red Lion, which should be on the shield of a knight, painted only on the signboard of an inn, remember all the great truths that you have read in this article; remember that this heraldic lion on the sign is the symbol of all that has lifted our Christian civilization into life and energy and honour—magnanimity, valour, a disdain of easy victories, a scorn for all the scorners of the weak.

The heraldic lion has, perhaps, sprawled rather too widely over this article. A great many other examples might be taken. The heraldic leopard is not without his good points. The dog-headed men in Africa were full of interest; nor must we forget Jehan de Mandeville's memorable description of a hippopotamus, that it was 'half man and half horse'. That is what may be called an impressionist or symbolist sketch of it; it avoids teasing details, and gives a sense of mass and atmosphere. I have often looked at the hippopotamus in his cage at the Zoological Gardens, and wondered which part of his appearance or physiognomy impressed the incisive Mandeville as being contributed by some human person of his acquaintance. Had he seen a very human

class of hippopotamus, or had he mixed with a hippo-
potamic class of men? But the general remarks which
I have made about the medieval lion, the heraldic lion,
apply equally well to all these other medieval monstrosities
or combinations. They were all fictitious. They were
all entirely different from and independent of, the living
creature upon which they were supposed to be modelled.
And those who wrote about them and talked about
them, and gravely disputed about all their charac-
teristics, physical, mental, and moral, were, at the bottom
of their hearts and the back of their minds, totally indifferent to whether they were true or not. The Middle
Ages were full of logic. And logic in its examples and
symbols is in its nature entirely indifferent to fact. It is as
easy to be logical about things that do not exist as about
things that do exist. If twice three is six, it is certain that
three men with two legs each will have six legs between
them. And if twice three is six, it is equally certain that three
men with two heads each will have six heads between
them. That there never were three men with two heads
each does not invalidate the logic in the least. It makes the
deduction impossible, but it does not make it illogical.
Twice three is still six, whether you reckon it in pigs or in
flaming dragons, whether you reckon it in cottages or in
castles-in-the-air. And the object of all this great medieval
and Renaissance science was simply to find everywhere
and anywhere examples of its philosophy. If the hippopotamus illustrated the idea of justice, well and good; if
it did not, so much the worse for the hippopotamus. These
ancients sought to make the brutes the mere symbol of
the man. Some moderns seek to make Man a mere symbol
of the brutes. These old scientists were only interested in
the human side of the beasts. Some new scientists are only
interested in the beastly side of the men. Instead of mak-

ing the ape and tiger mere accessories to the man, they make man a mere accessory, a mere afterthought to the ape and tiger. Instead of employing the hippopotamus to illustrate their philosophy, they employ the hippopotamus to make their philosophy, and the great fat books he writes you and I, please God, will never read.

THE COURT OF CAMELOT

SOMEBODY recently asked me what I meant by a reference to the myth of Arthur; or, rather, a reference to the myth of the myth of Arthur. For in my opinion it is only a modern myth that he is only an ancient one. The chief difference between ancient and modern times seems to be that formerly legends grew very slowly and now they grow very fast. The old legends generally grew more slowly and always had a more historical basis; and it seems to me overwhelmingly probable that the story of King Arthur had a very solid historical basis. This must in a sense be mere guesswork, for I am not competent to judge of the details; but I think I am as competent as anyone else to judge of the theories, in the sense of seeing whether they hang together and are inherently probable and consistent. Now the theory that treats Arthur entirely as a fairy-tale seems to me more fantastic than any fairy-tale. It sometimes takes the form of saying that there was some prehistoric Celtic god or other who afterwards came to be described in more detail as a king in Camelot. I have never been very clear, by the way, about how this vague transition from divinity to humanity is supposed to present itself to human nature. A particular story of an incarnate god or a fallen angel one can imagine easily enough. But I am a little confused about how the mere act of the Pimlico populace continually calling upon heaven in their human difficulties, would of itself become a story that a Mr Heaven had lived in a particular street in Pimlico. It seems rather more likely that a simple people would exaggerate a hero into a god, rather than deliberately diminish a god into a hero. But this is something of a side issue and I do not insist on it. Anyhow, they say there must have been a Celtic god and doubtless there was; doubtless there were many Celtic gods—too many Celtic gods for a fastidious monotheistic taste. I might respectfully inquire what had become of all the others; and why they have not all turned into Christian kings with orders of chivalry? And then the critics complete the confusion by saying, as a sort of after-thought, that Arthur may also have been the name of a king, but implying that this can have nothing to do with the idea of King Arthur.

Now all this seems to me mythical in the worst sense; that it is concentrated on myths and wholly careless of history. If we are studying a historical problem, it would be well to begin with the historical part of it; and if we want to know more, it is best to grasp what we know already. Now we do know as a historical fact that the beginning of the Dark Ages was a time when the north-west corner of the Roman Empire was ruined by barbarian invasions. We do know that those who successfully defended civilization everywhere became great legendary yet historic heroes and that in this respect the story of Arthur is just like the story of Alfred. There was certainly a legendary Alfred as well as a historical Alfred; and every common-sense comparison would lead one to think there was a historical Arthur as well as a legendary Arthur. But the question is one of proportion; and the saving of Christendom by the heroes of the Dark Ages does seem to me a sufficient cause for so huge a legend : the last trickle of tradition from some lost Welsh polytheism does not seem to me a sufficient cause. There are a dozen parallel cases of Christian heroes; there are not a dozen parallel cases of Welsh gods.

Then we come to the old suggestion that Arthur was

not Arthur but another person of the same name. Here
again people seem to forget that a legend requires a story
as well as a name. A legend is *about* something; it is not
started by a word but by some true or false event. The
earliest historical references to Arthur are references to
what he did. What he did was to defend Britain, as a
Christian and civilized State, against the heathen in-
vasion. The very first references to him deal with stories
like that of the Battle of Mount Badon, in which Arthur
drove the heathen before him and carried a holy image,
some say on his shield and some on his shoulders. If I
remember right, William of Malmesbury, soon after the
Norman Conquest, refers to Arthur not as a wild Welsh
demigod or even a doubtful Welsh saint, but as a solid
historical character whose name needs to be cleared from
the *later* accretions of Welsh fancy. Now there is no doubt
at all that battles similar to the Battle of Mount Badon
did in all sorts of countries stem or turn the tide of bar-
barism. There is no doubt whatever that when they did,
they left an enormous impression on the imaginations of
men, like a story of the Deluge or the Day of Judgement.
If the result was a myth, it was like some myth about a
man who had saved the sun and stars.

But there is another historical truth that is here forgotten. Many doubts about the Court of Camelot are
founded on the notion that anything so far back in time
must itself have been barbaric. The truth is, that, if it
was far enough back, it would almost certainly have been
civilized. It would have been in the last phase of the old
Roman civilization. The fallacy is like that of a man who
should say at daybreak that if it was darker four hours
before, it must have been darker still fourteen hours before. He would forget that fourteen hours might bring
him back into the previous day. And the fascination of

this study of the Dark Ages is precisely that the darkness does hide a buried day; the last lost daylight of the great culture of antiquity.

Much of the dullness of modern history came from the idea of progress. For history must be progress reversed. If things have always automatically grown brighter and better, then to trace things backwards is to go further and further not only into darkness but into dullness. It is to go from gold to lead and from lead to mud; from beautiful novelties to dreary negations. But, as a fact, these beautiful novelties have never appeared except when this negative theory of the past was itself negatived. They have come when people were quarrying in an older civilization, because it was more civilized than their own civilization. That is obviously what happened at the Renaissance, but it happened in many cases where it is less obvious. I believe that the peculiar magic and mastery still belonging to the Arthurian story is largely due to the long period during which men looked back to Roman Britain as something more rich and subtle and artistic than the barbarous centuries that succeeded it. They were not wrong in believing that Arthur and Lancelot were more courtly and cultured than Hengist and Horsa. If Arthur and Lancelot existed at all, they almost certainly were. The same has been true, of course, ever since people began to study the medieval civilization with any intelligence. Some sentimentalists in the eighteenth century may have begun by thinking ruined abbeys (especially by moonlight) merely interesting as rugged and barbaric, 'with shapeless sculpture decked'. But since we have begun to search out the scheme and science of medieval architecture, we have realized that it is the very reverse of barbaric, that it is especially organized and orderly. We have recognized that Gothic architecture was certainly not made by Goths;

and that the shapeless sculpture was anything but shape-less, and had a very deliberate shape. But we do not remember that, as we have groped for an understanding of the medieval system, so the men of the Dark Ages may well have groped for an understanding of the old Roman system. And it is natural that the last monuments of it should have appeared enormous in the twilight; and one of these monuments was the memory of Arthur.

WOLFE AND THE MIDSHIPMAN

THERE are people in the world who really hate the heroic. Granted that there is an extravagance always tending to overrate human achievements, there is an extravagance of triviality also, tending to underrate achievement, to take pleasure in a change from the poetic to the prosaic. That is why realistic novels are sometimes as interesting as romantic novels. It is simply because realistic novels are quite as arbitrary and fantastic as romantic novels. In the romance the hero is always jumping and perpetually falls on his feet. In the realistic story the hero is always plodding and perpetually falls on his nose. But in ordinary life it is unusual either to alight on a distant crag or to fall flat over a too proximate door-scraper. The romancer collects every instance of a beautiful triumph; the realist selects every case of an ugly cropper; but the bias of the realist is as extreme and as unscrupulous as that of the wildest romantic fabulist. If you throw enough mud, some of it will stick, especially to that unfortunate creature Man, who was originally made of mud. A realistic novel is written by stringing together all the tag-ends of human life—all the trains we miss, all the omnibuses we run after without catching, all the appointments that miscarry, and all the invitations that are declined; all the wasted half-hours at Clapham Junction, and all the infant prodigies that grow up into stupid men; all the rainy days and all the broken engagements; all the Might-Have-Beens and all the Hardly Weres. Realism is the art of connecting everything that is in its nature disconnected. But to do this properly a man must be a great artist and rather a good liar.

There are, then, partisans of the prosaic. They are not in the least facing life as it is : life as it is, is almost too splendid—nay, too beautiful to be faced. No man shall see life and live. They are making a special and personal selection, just as the aesthete or the optimist is making a special and personal selection. They nose about for the meannesses of mankind. They hunt for mortal humiliation. We know that they have this prosaic pugnacity in matters of fiction. But it is an interesting fact that they have it also about history. In history itself there is a school which may be called anti-romantic; and it is perpetually occupied in trying to explain away the many romances that have really happened.

When I was a boy I was told that General Wolfe before the assault on Quebec had recited the great lines of Gray about glory and the grave, and declared he would rather have written them than take Quebec. The story is a fine one, full of the eighteenth-century feeling of stoicism and heathen happiness before death, of the kinship of arts and arms, and of the soldier's splendid contempt for mere soldiering. When I was a man I was told to put away this childish legend and I put it away. It had been disproved. Wolfe had never said anything of the sort. And now, with a great jump, I read that the thing is substantially true after all.

I will take this story of General Wolfe and Gray's Elegy as a working instance of the way that the historical sceptics do the trick. They will discredit a story for which there is excellent evidence on the ground of certain omissions or discrepancies in that evidence. But they never make the least reference to whether these are of the kind that occur in true stories or of the kind that occur in false. Some slips are obviously the slips of a liar; other confusions arise in honest narration, and in honest narration alone. Some blunders prove falsehood; other blunders prove truth. Let us take this Quebec story and go into it a little.

The sceptics, it seems, begin by making the story manifestly ridiculous in order to deny it. 'Is it likely', they say, 'that General Wolfe would have quoted Gray while he was leading his troops in deadly silence to surprise the French?' Why, of course not; and nobody I ever heard of —certainly not I myself in my infancy—ever imagined that Wolfe talked about literature within earshot of the enemy; or selected the occasion of a steep and silent ascent to recite the whole of Gray's Elegy. Picture the soldiers crawling and clambering through the darkness hardly daring to pant too loud; and imagine the General putting his mouth to the ear of a midshipman and shouting in a hoarse whisper :

> The curfew tolls the knell of parting day,
> The lowing herd winds slowly o'er the lea,
> The ploughman homeward plods his weary way,
> And leaves the world to darkness and to me.
>
> Now fades the glimmering landscape on the sight—

—and all the rest of the verses. Of course Wolfe said it, if he ever said it at all, on some occasion previous to the actual assault—at some distance of time and place at which it was possible for people to speak out loud. Do the critics think that during the whole Canadian campaign the English soldiers conversed by talking on their fingers?

Well, the popular story is that some time before the assault, perhaps on the previous day, Wolfe recited a good part of the Elegy (chiefly the part about 'the paths of glory' and 'the grave') to a midshipman named Robinson. But, apparently, the only person who can be referred to was a Scotchman named Robison; which, of course, is a perfect example of the mistakes that only the truthful can make. Any ignorant Englishman, seeing the Scotch name Robison, might think it was merely a misprint for Robinson. As it does not matter a rap to the story whether his name was Robinson or Rehoboam, of course men would tell the tale in its familiar form. If there is in Westmorland a person whose name is spelt Smiph, he must not complain if he is turned into Smith in stories in which he is a secondary figure. If there is in North Cornwall a fine old family of Jomes, it will probably become Jones for the purposes of popular narrative. Those are things which are modified, not in order to complicate a fraud, but in order to simplify the truth. And it is the whole case against the pedantic opponents of the romantic element in history that they do not seem able to distinguish between this instinctive omission of the irrelevant, which is simply the art of telling stories, and the introduction of ingenious and over-elaborate detail which is the whole art of telling lies. If popular traditions change, it is rather by dropping things out than by putting things in. The story grows simpler through the ages, not more complex.

Then the massive sceptical mind moves on to the next great difficulty in the story. Not only is it the awful truth that the midshipman Robinson was really Robison, but he was not really a midshipman. 'Robison was rated as a midshipman in accordance with the usual convention that gives every gentleman employed on a ship of war an official rank, as he was afterwards rated as a colonel when Professor of Mathematics in the C. Cadet Corps at St Petersburg.' Now, these are very interesting facts, but the insistence on them seems again to betray a singular ignorance of the way in which an honest man tells a true story. A man says, 'Wolfe said to a midshipman.' He does not say, 'Wolfe said to a person rated as a midshipman in accordance with the usual convention that gives to every gentleman employed on a ship of war an official rank, as he was afterwards rated as a colonel when Professor of Mathematics in the C. Cadet Corps at St Petersburg.' I can quite imagine Mrs Nickleby telling the story in that way, but nobody else.

It does not affect the story in the slightest degree whether Mr Robison was a midshipman, or a music-master, or a boot-black, or an Ethiopian king, or a person rated as a midshipman in accordance with the usual convention which gives, &c. But it does affect that story that we should get to the story with some reasonable speed and hear what was said by Wolfe, the only person in whom we are interested at all. Therefore, of course, the popular narrator said 'midshipman', simply because one can say 'midshipman' quicker than one can say 'Jack Robinson' or 'Jack Robison'.

ABOUT CHRISTIANITY

A CURIOUS chance led me lately to stumble over an incident which happened some time ago. It was concerned with one of the most interesting men of our time; and also one of the problems which are peculiar to our civilization and our time. I give the story as I heard it; it reflects on nobody, whether it is true or untrue.

It seems that Mr Eric Gill, the distinguished sculptor, was engaged to erect a sculptural memorial for the League of Nations, expressing that need for Peace which is now the most direct and vital, not to say deadly, necessity, for all Christians and for all sane men. Apparently he planned a design which involved a Christian symbol; and this was resisted, on the ground that non-Christians might not accept it. I suspect that it was not so much a question of the non-Christians outside Europe as of the Anti-Christians inside Europe. It is very unlike all the little I know of the intellectual leaders of those who follow Confucius or Buddha to object especially to a mystical emblem connected with Christ; and nobody supposes that anybody except leaders and intellectuals has very much to say in such modern political problems. And as for Islam, it is enough to say that Christ is already given at least as high a place by all Moslems as He is by many Modernists.

What produces a practical embarrassment in this case is the sincere and savage hatred felt by many Europeans for the religion of their own European past. And this interests me, simply as a historical comparison, because it is really a historical curiosity. It is a difficulty quite peculiar to Christendom. There does not seem to have been anything like it in Paganism. In the last phase of Paganism there was every sort of doubt; there was every sort of denial; but there was not this particular sort of difficulty. The old gods were once perhaps really worshipped as gods; they were then enjoyed as legends; they were even treated lightly as jokes; but they were never hated as symbols. There may have been a time, though I rather doubt it, when people did actually believe that Apollo drove a golden chariot through the sky; but, anyhow, long after Apollo had become an abstraction, an allegory of music or poetry, a tradition that nobody but the most remote rustics took quite seriously, there was most certainly no sculptor from one end of the Roman Empire to the other who would have felt any difficulty, or found any difficulty, in carving Apollo as driving a chariot. The heathens grew cold towards their religion, or even contemptuous of their religion, but they never had any irritation against it that could make them refuse to use its images, or its imagery, in the realm of imagination.

There must have been multitudes of intellectuals, living on the tradition of Euripides or Lucian, who took even a bitter or mocking or pessimistic view of the gods; or simply thought there were no such things as gods in the world; but they would never have objected to gods as graven images. I never heard of any case of any heathen sceptics becoming iconoclasts; and going out and smashing the popular deities as a protest on behalf of abstract truth. They accepted the lyre of Apollo or the wand of Mercury, just as we still accept a Cupid on a Valentine or a nymph on a stone fountain. We may say that the cupid has been vulgarized and is no longer truly a god. We may say that the nymph has met the gorgon, and been turned to stone. And they may have known in their hearts that their religion was dead. But because it was dead, they had even less desire to make exhausting efforts to kill it. If Christianity were really one of the cults studied in comparative religion, if it were really, as its critics sometimes say, a thing made up of materials borrowed from Paganism, if it were really only the last myth or ritual of the long undying death of the Roman Empire, then there is no reason why its symbolism should not be used forever by anybody; as the symbolism of nymphs and cupids is still used forever by anybody. The real reason is that this religion does differ in one detail from all those ancient and beautiful religions. It is not dead. Everybody knows in his heart that it is not dead; and none better than those who want it to die.

The people arranging for the Peace Memorial of the League of Nations would not have the slightest objection to covering it with signs and symbols which were once religious. They would not object to a statue of Peace holding the olive branch like a statue of Minerva; they would not object to a symbolic figure of Sunrise which had the lyre or the horses of Apollo; they would not be annoyed if somebody conceived womanhood under the form of Diana hunting or manhood under the form of Hercules at rest. All these things are now really an allegory. And if Christians could accept so trifling a modernist modification of their view as to agree that Christianity is dead, they could safely go on using all their great historical and hagiological wealth of imagery and illustration; and nobody would object to ten thousand angels or a million martyrs or any number of crosses and haloes. But the ground of the resistance is that the whole modern comparison between the decline of Paganism and the decline of Christianity is false. Paganism, in the historic sense of Polytheism, did decline once and for all. Christianity has declined twenty times; but nobody who hated it was ever quite certain that it was dead. The rationalist historians of the nineteenth century found it easy to trace in a curve the rise and fall of a religion. They showed very lucidly, to their own satisfaction, that such a historical monstrosity was first a myth, and then a superstition, and then a tradition, and then an abstraction and an allegory. And what they wrote was largely true, if they had happened to be writing the history of Jupiter-Ammon. But as a history of post-Pagan Europe, commonly called Christendom, it is simply not true. It is not the story of something that ruled the whole world, as a pagan deity ruled the whole city. It is not the story of something which was lost when a man left his own city, and enlarged his mind by considering the gods of other cities. It did not begin by being so powerful as Paganism; it never came to being so impotent as Paganism. It was the story of something that was unsafe at its safest and living still at its lowest; something which is always coming out of the Catacombs and going back again; something that is never entirely acceptable when it appears; and never entirely forgotten when it disappears.

It is this utterly unique and even unnatural vigilance that can alone explain a difficulty like that raised about the graven image of Peace. It is that even in proclaiming political peace it proclaims spiritual war. Its things cannot be used as dead things to deck out any alien triumph; we will not be the skeleton at any pagan feast or the corpse for any scientific body-snatching. But, quite apart from our various individual views on such questions of philosophy, there remains a very practical problem of history. These mysteries are the background of the modern European's past, just as those myths were the background of the most sceptical Pagan's past. And the matter can be put to a perfectly practical test. If you had told one of the last Greek sculptors that he must not represent anything out of the great Greek myths, he would probably have answered, 'What shall I represent?' These things were the whole imagery of his imagination. If you tell an artist of the Christian culture, whatever his opinions, that he is to represent peace or charity or universal love by a familiar and obvious emblem—what is the poor devil to do? Pause and think of that point; for it is a perfectly practical point. What *are* the popular emblems of peace, if we are to cut out all that comes from myths or mysteries or the past?

ST GEORGE FOR ENGLAND

I AM informed on fairly good authority that the day upon which I write these words is St George's Day. It is very characteristic of our country that we make far more fuss about St Patrick's Day than we do about St George's. It is a part of that curious elephantine modesty of the English in some matters : a modesty so heavy and helpless that foreigners mistake it for pride. It is true that within recent years there have been some signs in us of mere boasting. But even they are mainly glorifications of things that are not strictly ourselves; things that, as a general rule, we know nothing about—such as Australia. Even when the English do brag they seem to brag of anything except England. Something prevents us from becoming poetical and dithyrambic about ourselves. Some people will tell you that this is because we are so stern and practical, but that is all talk, and un-English talk at that. As a matter of fact, we are not nearly so practical as we were when we were much more dithyrambic. I do not know why it is, but the English really have got a certain kind of embarrassment and dislike of show; but whatever it is, it certainly is not because they are not sufficiently romantic; their magnificent romantic literature can answer for that; for they are (I think) the only nation in the world whose absolutely first-class literature is rather romantic than classical. Sometimes I think that the Englishman is undemonstrative because he is much too romantic to be demonstrative. Like all sentimentalists, he is secretive.

He does not tell you his feelings because they are too romantic to tell.

But the neglect of St George is an example of that lack of animated ritual which Irishmen or Italians in judging us mistake for a vital lack of romance. It may be urged by some that the neglect of St George (as compared, for instance, with St Patrick) may be easily explained by the fact that the historical St Patrick was a great man whose life is largely known and whose work can be definitely admired; whereas the historical St George is chiefly remarkable for having no history. We know nothing about his life and only one thing about his death, that he was martyred for the faith. For I suppose that everyone has realized that Gibbon, in identifying the saint with the fraudulent financier who was an Arian and bore the same name, was merely letting his anti-Christian enthusiasm run away with him and wallowing in the charming thought of a saint who rigged the market. To suppose that that amiable financier could ever have become the patron saint of England is to misunderstand the whole atmosphere not merely of the morals, but of the theology and hagiology of the early Church. I take it then that the historic St George, if there was one at all (to which I am extremely indifferent), was the Christian of whom we know nothing but his death.

But those who suggest that the remote and impersonal quality in the historic St George accounts for the English indifference to him know little of patron saints or of the essential nature of saint-worship. Saint-worship is not the same as hero-worship; it is a much less dangerous thing than hero-worship. For hero-worship generally means the absorption or transmutation of some part, at any rate, of one's own original ideas of goodness under the heat and hypnotism of some strong personality. But saint-worship, especially when it is a worship of saints whom we know little or nothing about, is simply the worship of that tradition of goodness in which the saint's name has been embalmed; and into that empty mould our own natural idealism can much more easily be poured. The invocation of saints is much less idolatrous than the invocation of historical heroes after the manner of Carlyle. For you can only admire the goodness of the saint, whereas you may come to admire the badness of the hero. You may get all kinds of dangerous bias and sophistry and bad advice from the man in history whom you know something about. You can get nothing but good advice from the man you know nothing about. Thus, to take the historical St George; if all we know about him is that he was killed for his opinions, that fact is, properly considered, so staggering that it might send us all singing into battle. Or take rather the legendary St George, who is (I need hardly say) very much more important than the real one. As it is, St George the dragon-slayer stands to us simply and sufficiently as the symbol of courage. He does not stand in our minds connected with any of those silly epigrams which great men in their old age utter to misguided youth. St George never told anybody what was his 'method' or what was 'the secret of his power'. He made no remarks, he merely killed the dragon. He did not say that the dragon was killed on Eton playing-fields. He did not say that he had never met a dragon with whom he couldn't do a deal. He never called the death of the dragon inevitable; while he was fighting the dragon he had thoroughly discovered that it was not. He never said that the way to kill a dragon was to work hard in early youth, or to start with twopence a day, or to avoid tobacco, or to know your own mind, or any of those inane tips. For St George knew very well what all real soldiers know; that the only way to be even approximately likely to kill a dragon is to give the dragon a heavy chance of killing you. And this method, which is the only one, is much too unpleasant to be talked about. You see, I am making a character of St George at my own will and fancy. That is the whole point and advantage of the unknown saint. That is why saint-worship is so much more free than hero-worship.

I think myself that something might be done by the English nation with the legend of St George and the Dragon. It has still a lingering hold on the people in some counties, where the mummers at Christmas or Easter still perform a rude drama in which the English champion overcomes the evil principle in single combat. In almost all these little ritual plays, so far as I have noticed, the same singular and picturesque episode occurs. I mean that when the arch-enemy (sometimes the Dragon, sometimes a Turkish Knight, sometimes some other alien figure) is thrown to the ground by St George, he always calls out for a doctor. A doctor is always provided by the Christian conqueror, and the fight recommences. This episode might be made to mean a great deal if any English poet philosophized the legend of St George, as Goethe philosophized the legend of Faust. For it is true that the chivalrous and Christian character (which St George typifies) fights under that disadvantage of the doctor. He has to contend at once against the mercilessness of his enemy and the mercifulness of himself. But again the legendary drama is right when it makes St George conquer. When modern cynics (utterly ignorant of courage and, therefore, utterly ignorant of war) say that we must be more brutal if we are to be efficient, they forget that the most brutal civilizations are the least efficient. Oriental nations that torture their captives are themselves captive. Savages that eat men do not seem to thrive on it. Our European civilization has faults enough, but it is on the whole the most merciful and it is on the whole the most strong. For the mind that can imagine sufferings is the same that can imagine a new gun.

THE NATIONAL ANTHEM

I SEE that there is a movement in many influential quarters for cutting out the best verse in the National Anthem. This is very typical of many of our 'reforms' that arise out of a sense of refinement and not out of a sense of right. When I say the best verse, I mean the one that confounds the tricks of all the enemies of the State. And I call it the best verse because, in a work that no one particularly praises or preserves for literary reasons, it is the most quaintly national, the most unique, the most sincere and vigorous, and by far the most democratic. One does not hold up 'God Save the King' as a poem like the 'Mariners of England', any more than one holds up the picture of John Bull as something beautiful and well-proportioned, like the St George of Donatello. The thing is a patriotic curiosity; and the most curious and patriotic part of it is exactly the part that these people want to cut out. And, ethically, it is excellent.

> Confound their politics,
> Frustrate their knavish tricks,

may not be very good poetry, but it is very good, sound Christian morals. If there are any knavish tricks, I hope we all pray they may be frustrated. And as for confounding politics, a good many of us have been in sympathy with the idea ever since we made a study of the ways of the confounded politicians. The poem does not define the people denounced, except in so far that they are the enemies of the King, who is in all such symbolic songs made a symbol of the commonwealth. I happen to think that the King's worst enemies often sit at his own Council-board, and that England's worst invaders and destroyers often have the high places in the senate; but all this does not prevent me from singing the anthem with heartiness and relish.

What the refined people (confound their knavish tricks!) will not see is that, if you are loyal to anything and wish to preserve it, you must recognize that it has or might have enemies; and you must hope that the enemies will fail. The real insolence, if there were any, would lie in saying, 'God save the King'—in calling the Universal and Eternal to take care of a particular tribal chief on a trivial little island. But undoubtedly, if you have a right to ask God to save him, you have a right to ask God to frustrate those who seek to destroy him; the two sentences simply mean the same thing. The oblivion of so obvious a fact is only a part of that foolish forgetfulness of the real ethics of fighting which is equally perilous today, whether it takes its Jingo or its Pacifist form. Not only is the army the chief business of our processions; but processions seem to be considered the chief business of the army. From no point of view ought armaments to be ornaments. I have no respect for that chronic war-fever, or love of conquest, which (as the phrase goes) draws the sword and throws away the scabbard. But I have even less respect for that arrogant etiquette that keeps the scabbard when it has thrown away the sword. And among the results of this masquerade style of militarism is a neglect of the most naked and structural principles of fighting.

Nothing is baser in our time than the idea that we can have special enthusiasms for things, so long as they are secure, without pledging ourselves to uphold them if they are ever in peril. You cannot have a devotion that is not a

F

boundary. You cannot have a boundary that is not a barricade. If you do not think mankind a sacred brotherhood to be everywhere saluted and saved, then do not say so. But if you do say so, then you must certainly be ready to save it from sharks or tigers, from monsters or from microbes. If you do not think your nation a solid entity and a holy soil, then do not call it your nation. But if you do, you must admit that it might be as much hated by others as it is loved by you. If it is really individual, it is just as likely to be hated as it is to be loved.

There is another obvious moral ground upon which we should continue to 'confound their politics'. The refined people (confound, &c.) seem to think that there is something unpleasant and profane about making a war religious. I should say that there ought to be no war except religious war. If war is irreligious, it is immoral. No man ought ever to fight at all unless he is prepared to put his quarrel before that invisible Court of Arbitration with which all religion is concerned. Unless he thinks he is vitally, eternally, cosmically in the right, he is wrong to fire off a pocket-pistol. If he does think he is in the right, he is surely justified in praying that the right may prevail. The separation between war and the Church, like the separation between business and the Chapel, would only mean that the religion would grow much too thin, while the cynicism would grow much too fat. It would be a good thing if religion thought a little more about this world—and if politics thought a little more about the other.

And lastly, no one seems to notice that this verse of the National Anthem (if my memory serves me right) is the only one that contains the popular note of comradeship as well as the popular note of conflict. I quote from memory, but I think the verse runs—

O Lord, our God, arise,
Scatter his enemies,
And make them fall.
Confound their politics,
Frustrate their knavish tricks;
On Thee our hopes we fix :
God save us all.

It is the only verse that begins with something like fine
Biblical diction, as of a whirlwind rising. It is the only
verse that ends with a universal and democratic bene-
diction. I do not wonder that the Moderns want it
removed.

KING GEORGE IV

I HAVE just been reading what is not only a very excellent biography, but a very much-needed book. It is a study of 'George the Fourth' by Mr Shane Leslie. It is in no sense what even shallow people would call a whitewashing of George IV, though it is the restoration of a blackened portrait. It has not the tone of an advocate for the defence any more than for the prosecution. But it is a criticism of the critics of George. And it is a very damaging criticism too.

The truth is that poor George has been the victim of a prolonged effort of Propaganda. It was partly Whig and partly Victorian propaganda. But because it went on for a very long time and enlisted many literary men of what may be called the Whig patronage, it has come to seem to many of my generation and the next a normal truth of English history. It is quite obvious that, long before we come to the really fine qualities of the man, even his ordinary qualities were caricatured in the most unscrupulous and scandalous fashion. In weakness and in strength he was very much of a man—of what we call a man's man. He has not only been represented as a ladies' man—which perhaps he was; he has been talked of as a lady-killer almost in the literal sense of Bluebeard. The truth is that George's conduct, while wrong by a Christian standard, was very far from being exceptionally wrong by the ordinary heathen standard of hundreds of such men of the world. Very few of those men have risked so much as he did for the one heroic love of his life; and, if he had risked more, he might well have been called a hero.

74

But he was not a hero; he was a very human being; a man, but not a monster. Yet it certainly is as a monster, swollen, bloated, and abominable, that he haunted even our nurseries like a nightmare.

A coincidence of two causes, I think, produced this lurid transformation and tradition. The first was aristocratic and the second democratic; and together they turned both the Whig and the Radical against the King's memory. The first was that he had been in every sense, and even remained in some sense, a Radical himself. At least he was once a Liberal even with a large 'L', and was always a liberal with a small one. But he had changed sides in the ordinary party sense, and joined in the ordinary shuffling and inconsistency of the party system. The Whigs hated him for having been a Whig more than for being a Tory. But the aristocrats who had known him knew he was intelligent; knew he had understood what he was doing and what he was undoing. His very intelligence let him in for a charge of intellectual treason. That was the sort of monster he was—a constitutional monarch who could not act for himself, and yet could think for himself.

The second cause that coincides with this was the genuine popular legend of the pathos and innocence of Queen Caroline. Now about that the King may have been wrong, but he certainly was not inhumanly or inconceivably wrong; and the wrong certainly was not all on one side. George was really wrong not in divorcing Caroline, but in marrying Caroline. In divorcing her, as a matter of fact, he was simply ceasing to be a bigamist. For he was already married to a much better woman. But the mob has a mysterious sort of power of hitting the right nail with the wrong hammer. George was very properly pelted for being false to his wife; only he was really being false to quite another wife. Anyhow, his popularity with posterity was killed by those two combining forces. It was killed by the horror of the populace who knew nothing about him, and the jealousy of the gentry who knew too much about him. But the time has come when a more rational and reliable estimate can be made than was possible to the Whig tradition which Thackeray inherited from Macaulay; and with admirable wit, sympathy, and compact criticism, Mr Shane Leslie has made it.

In truth, there is a great deal to praise in George IV. At any rate, there was a very great deal to praise in the Prince Regent. It was not entirely his fault if there was less to praise in the King than there had been in the Prince. If ever a man's life was broken and brutally mismanaged by other people, it was his. His father was a fool who repeatedly relieved the monotony of that fact by becoming a lunatic. If anything, he was quieter and less mischievous as a lunatic than he was as a fool. He pestered and oppressed his children, and drove them into dark and devious ways. Yet even here there is a good example of the way in which the world is unjust to the Prince Regent. It has often been repeated that he wanted his child to be trained to be truthful, and admitted that he had fallen into lax ways in such matters, through the false position into which the old family tyranny had forced him in his youth. This is used as evidence against him— that he had himself confessed to being a liar. But no real liar ever confesses to being a liar. The confession is not a proof of how false he was, but of how candid he was.

He was forbidden by bigots and tyrants to call his wife his wife, and that is a situation which no man's sense of honour will ever perfectly survive. It broke George's career across the middle; and the second half was a crippled thing. Yet even as a cripple he did things that the active and ambitious around him did not think of doing. Mr Shane Leslie, among his many admirable phrases, uses one that is especially vivid and veracious; George had 'a fierce streak of humanity'. His acts of mercy were abrupt, angry, and even militant. They had the flash of finality; they were absolute renunciations or abject apologies. He was devoted to pugilism; but when a pugilist was killed in the ring at Brighton he took a vow never to see a prize-fight again. He had a profoundly Christian hatred of the callous spirit in the criminal law, which executes men as if by clockwork, and he paved the world with pardons for condemned men. He pardoned them *not* in a patronizing and facile fashion, as much meaner enemies have implied, but, on the contrary, with vigilance and vivid worry and a sort of insomnia of responsibility. He sat up all night looking for a loophole in the law by which he could let some obscure criminal free. He took trouble in exactly the type of cases in which most men (especially men of his position) would never think of taking it. He happened to turn down a street where a man stood in pillory for a political offence—having, indeed, been put there by the police and the lawyers for a libel upon George himself. George was so much distressed at the thought that he might conceivably be supposed to have triumphed ungenerously over his slanderer that he wrote a personal letter apologizing for the 'indelicacy' of his conduct. A man moved in such a case to such an apology ought not to be called, merely with a sneer, the First Gentleman of Europe.

George's liberality was anything but a mere party pose and the making of a cabal against his father. He was liberal about the very things on which most party Whigs were not liberal at all—for instance, he sympathized with the point of view of the Irish. If he could have come to the throne with his real wife as a Queen, it is possible that the whole tragedy of a hundred years might have been averted. There are a great many good things that might have happened if the younger and more generous George could have become a normal and national King. There is nothing that can be done now except do reasonable justice to his memory; and it was long before anybody thought of doing it. But nobody who reads Mr Shane Leslie's lively and pointed paragraphs has any excuse for thinking that Thackeray exhausted the subject or that there is no picture of George except in the cartoons of Gilray. He will know well enough that the man who kept a complete set of Jane Austen in each of his houses, that he might read at any moment, was not a coarse and comic drunkard understanding nothing but bruisers and cock-fighting. He will know that the man who endangered his crown out of chivalrous devotion to a devout and religious woman was not an utterly selfish satyr whose very appetite was cold. He will know that the friend of Fox and Sheridan cannot possibly have been a mere dummy dressed up as a dandy; and that the man whom Canning and Castlereagh often thought too clever for them can hardly have been entirely a fool.

KING EDWARD VII

I

On the very night that King Edward died, it happened that the present writer experienced some of those trivialities that can bring about one's head all the terrors of the universe. The shocking news was just loose in London, but it had not touched the country where I was, when a London editor attempted to tell me the truth by telephone. But all the telephones in England were throbbing and thundering with the news; it was impossible to clear the line; and it was impossible to hear the message. Again and again I heard stifled accents saying something momentous and unintelligible; it might have been the landing of the Germans or the end of the world. With the snatches of this strangled voice in my ears I went into the garden and found, by another such mystical coincidence, that it was a night of startling and blazing stars—stars so fierce and close that they seemed crowding round the roof and tree-tops. White-hot and speechless they seemed striving to speak, like that voice that had been drowned amid the drumming wires. I know not if any reader has ever had a vigil with the same unreasoning sense of a frustrated apocalypse. But if he has, he will know one of the immortal moods out of which legends rise and he will not wonder that men have joined the notion of a comet with the death of a King.

But besides this historic stroke, this fall of a national monument, there is also the loss of a personality. Over and above the dark and half-superstitious suggestion that the fate of our country has turned a corner and entered a new epoch, there is the pathetic value of the human epoch that has just closed. The starting-point for all study of King Edward is the fact of his unquestionable and positive popularity. I say positive, because most popularity is negative; it is no more than toleration. Many an English landlord is described as popular among his tenants, when the phrase only means that no tenant hates him quite enough to be hanged for putting a bullet in him. Or, again, in milder cases, a man will be called a popular administrator because his rule, being substantially successful, is substantially undisturbed; some system works fairly well and the head of the system is not hated, for he is hardly felt. Quite different was the practical popularity of Edward VII. It was a strictly personal image and enthusiasm. The French, with their talent for picking the right word, put it best when they described King Edward as a kind of universal uncle. His popularity in poor families was so frank as to be undignified; he was really spoken of by tinkers and tailors as if he were some gay and prosperous member of their own family. There was a picture of him upon the popular retina infinitely brighter and brisker than there is of any politician. There was something in him that appealed to those strange and silent crowds that are invisible because they are enormous. In connexion with him the few voices that really sound popular, sound also singularly loyal. Since his death was declared there have already been many written and spoken eulogies.

If you dig deep enough into any ancient ceremony, you will find the traces of that noble truism called democracy, which is not the latest but the earliest of human ideas. Just as in the very oldest part of an English church you will unearth the level bricks of the Romans, so in the very oldest part of every royal or feudal form you will unearth the level laws of the Republic. In that complex and loaded rite of Coronation, which King Edward underwent, there is distinct trace of the ancient idea of a King being elected like a President. The Archbishop shows the King to the assembled people and asks if he is accepted or refused. Edward VII, like other modern Kings, went through a ritual election by an unreal mob. But if it had been a real election by a real mob—he would still have been elected. That is the really important point for democrats.

The largeness of the praise of King Edward in the popular legend was fundamentally due to this, that he was a leader in whom other men could see themselves. The King's interest in sport, good living, and Continental travel was exactly of the kind that every clerk or commercial traveller could feel in himself on a smaller scale and in a more thwarted manner. Now, it emphatically will not do to dismiss this popular sympathy in pleasure as the mere servile or vulgar adoration of a race of snobs. To begin with, mere worldly rank could not and did not achieve such popularity for Ernest Duke of Cumberland or Alfred Duke of Edinburgh or even for the Prince Consort; and to go on with mere angry words like snobbishness is an evasion of the democratic test. I fancy the key to the question is this; that, in an age of prigs and dehumanized humanitarians, King Edward stood to the whole people as the emblem of this ultimate idea—that however extraordinary a man may be by office, influence, or talent, we have a right to ask that the extraordinary man should be also an ordinary man. He was more representative than representative government; he was the whole theme of Walt Whitman—the average man enthroned.

His reputation for a humane normality had one aspect

in which he was a model to philanthropists. Innumerable tales were told of his kindness or courtesy, ranging from the endowment of a children's hospital to the offer of a cigar, from the fact that he pensioned a match-seller to the mere fact that he took off his hat. But all these tales took the popular fancy all the more because he himself was the kind of man to share the pleasures he distributed. His offer of a cigar was the more appreciated because he offered himself a cigar as well. His taking off his hat was the more valued because he himself was by no means indifferent to decent salutations or discourteous slights. Philanthropists too frequently forget that pity is quite a different thing from sympathy; for sympathy means suffering with others and not merely being sorry that they suffer. If the strong brotherhood of men is to abide, if they are not to break up into groups alarmingly like different species, we must keep this community of tastes in giver and received. We must not only share our bread, but share our hunger.

King Edward was a man of the world and a diplomatist; but there was nothing of the aristocrat about him. He had a just sense of the dignity of his position; but it was very much such a sense as a middle-class elective magistrate might have had, a Lord Mayor or the President of a Republic. It was even in a sense formal, and the essence of aristocracy is informality. It is no violation of the political impartiality of the Crown to say that he was, in training and tone of mind, liberal. The one or two points on which he permitted himself a partisan attitude were things that he regarded as common-sense emancipations from mere custom, such as the Deceased Wife's Sister Bill. Both in strength and weakness he was international; and it is undoubtedly largely due to him that we have generally dropped the fashion of systematically and doggedly misunderstanding the great civilization of France. But the first and last thought is the same : that there are millions in England who have hardly heard of the Prime Minister to whom King Edward was a picture of paternal patriotism; and in the dark days that lie before us it is, perhaps, just those millions who may begin to move.

II

The calamity of the King's death was unofficially acknowledged almost before it was officially acknowledged. The people were prompter in mourning than the officers of state in bidding them mourn. The national mourning—taken as a whole, of course—is all the more universal for being irregular, all the more unanimous for being scrappy or even intermittent. Armies of retainers clad in complete black, endless processions of solemn robes and sable plumes, could not be a quarter so impressive as the cheap black band of a man in corduroys or the cheap black hat of a girl in pink and magenta. The part is greater than the whole. Nevertheless, the formal side of funeral customs, as is right and natural, is already engaging attention. Sir William Richmond, always prominent in any question of the relation of art to public life, has already sketched out a scheme of mortuary decoration so conceived as to avoid the inhuman monotony of black. He would have a sombre, but still rich, scheme of colour, of Tyrian purple, dim bronze, and gold. Both artistically and symbolically, there is much that is sound in the conception. Indeed, Sir William Richmond, consciously or unconsciously, is in this matter following an ecclesiastical tradition. The world mourns in black, but the Church

mourns in violet—one of the many instances of the fact
that the Church is a much more cheerful thing than the
world. Nor is the difference an idle accident; it really
corresponds by chasms of spiritual separation. Black is
dark with absence of colour; violet is dark with density
and combination of colour; it is at once as blue as mid-
night and as crimson as blood. And there is a similar
distinction between the two ideas of death, between the
two types of tragedy. There is the tragedy that is founded
on the worthlessness of life; and there is the deeper
tragedy that is founded on the worth of it. The one sort
of sadness says that life is so short that it can hardly
matter; the other that life is so short that it matters for
ever.

But though in this, as in many other matters, it is
religion alone that retains any tradition of a freer and
more humane popular taste, it may well be doubted
whether in the present instance the existing popular
taste should not be substantially gratified, or, at least,
undisturbed. King Edward was not the kind of man in
whose honour we should do even beautiful things that are
in any sense eccentric. His sympathies in all such matters
were very general sympathies; he stood to millions of
people as the very incarnation of common-sense, social
adaptability, tact, and a rational conventionality. His
people delighted in the million snapshots of him in shoot-
ing-dress at a shooting-box, or in racing clothes at a race-
meeting, in morning-dress in the morning or in evening-
dress in the evening, because all these were symbols of a
certain sensible sociability and readiness for everything
with which they loved to credit him. For it must always
be remembered in this connexion that masculine costume
is different at root from feminine costume—different in its
whole essence and aim. It is not merely a question of the

man dressing in dull colours or the woman in bright; it is a question of the object. A Life Guardsman has very splendid clothes; an artistic lady may have very dingy clothes. But the point is that the Life Guard only puts on his bright clothes so as to be like other Life Guards. But the artistic lady always seeks to have some special, delicate, and exquisite shade of dinginess different from the dinginess of other artistic ladies. Though gleaming with scarlet and steel, the Life Guard is really invisible. Though physically, no doubt, of terrific courage, he is morally cowardly, like nearly all males. Like the insects that are as green as the leaves or the jackals that are as red as the desert, a man generally seeks to be unseen by taking the colour of his surroundings, even if it be a brilliant colour. A female dress is a dress; a male dress is a uniform. Men dress smartly so as not to be noticed; but all women dress to be noticed—gross and vulgar women to be grossly and vulgarly noticed, wise and modest women to be wisely and modestly noticed.

Now, of this soul in masculine 'good form', this slight but genuine element of a manly modesty in conventions, the public made King Edward a typical and appropriate representative. They like to think of him appearing as a soldier among soldiers, a sailor among sailors, a Freemason at his Lodge, or a Peer among his Peers. For this reason they even tolerated the comic idea of his being a Prussian Colonel when he was in Prussia; and they took a positive pleasure in the idea of his being a Parisian boulevardier when he was in Paris. Since he was thus a public symbol of the more generous and fraternal uses of conventionality, we may be well content with a conventional scheme of mourning; especially when in this case, as in not a few other cases, the conventional merely means the democratic. King Edward's popularity was such a very popular kind of popularity that it would be rather more appropriate to make his funeral vulgar than to make it aesthetic. It is true that legend connects his name with two or three attempts to modify the ungainliness and gloom of our modern male costume; but he hardly insisted on any of them, and none of them was of a kind specially to satisfy Sir William Richmond. The aesthetes might perhaps smile on the notion of knee breeches; but I fear that brass buttons on evening coats would seem to them an aggravation of their wrong. Even where King Edward was an innovator, he was an innovator along popular and well-recognized lines; a man who would have liked a funeral to be funereal, as he would have liked a ball to be gay. We need not, therefore, feel it so very inappropriate even if in the last resort the celebrations are in the most humdrum or even jog-trot style, if they satisfy the heart of the public, though not the eye of the artist.

And yet again, in connexion with those aspects of the late King which may be and are approved on more serious and statesmanlike grounds (as, for instance, his international attitude towards peace), this value of a working convention can still be found. It is easy to say airily, in an ethical textbook or a debating club resolution, that Spaniards should love Chinamen, or that Highlanders should suddenly embrace Hindus. But, as men are in daily life, such brotherhood is corrupted and confused, though never actually contradicted. It is the fundamental fact that we are all men; but there are circumstances that permit us to feel it keenly and other circumstances that almost prevent us from feeling it at all. It is here that convention (which only means a coming together) makes smooth the path of primal sympathy, and by getting people, if only for an hour, to act alike, begins to make them feel alike. I have said much against aristocracy and shall continue to do so, but I will never deny that aristocracy has certain queer advantages, not very often mentioned. One of them is that which affects European diplomacy : that a gentleman is the same all over Europe, while a peasant or even a merchant, may be very different. A Dutch gentleman and an Irish gentleman stand on a special and level platform; a Dutch peasant and an Irish peasant are divided by all dynastic and divine wars. Of course, this means that a peasant is superior to a gentleman—more genuine, more historic, more national; but that, surely, is obvious. Nevertheless, for cosmopolitan purposes, such as diplomacy, a gentleman may be used— with caution. And the reason that has made aristocrats effective as diplomatists is the same that made King Edward effective; the existence of a convention or convenient form that is understood everywhere and makes action and utterance easy for everyone. Language itself is only an enormous ceremony. King Edward completely understood that nameless Volapuk or Esperanto on which modern Europe practically reposes. He never put himself in a position that Europe could possibly misunderstand, as the Kaiser did by his theocratic outbursts, even if they were logical; or the Tsar by his sweeping repressions, even if they were provoked. Partly a German, by blood, partly a Frenchman, by preference, inter-married with all the thrones of Europe and quite conscious of their very various perplexities, he had the right to be called a great citizen of Europe. There are only two things that can bind men together; a convention and a creed. King Edward was the last, the most popular, and probably the most triumphant example of Europe combining with success upon a large and genial convention. Tact and habit and humanity had in him their final exponent in

G

all the Courts, reviews, race-courses, and hotels of Christendom. If these are not enough, if it is not found sufficient for Europe to have a healthy convention, then Europe must once more have a creed. The coming of the creed will be a terrible business.

KING GEORGE V

THE passing of King George the Fifth from the scene of his labours, labours admittedly among the most devoted and unselfish of the public duties of our time, marks in more ways than one a special achievement in our national history. It is self-evident, and has therefore been said by many and seen by all, that through all this lifetime the English Crown has remained popular and secure, in a time when Crowns were falling on every side. But the remotest rim of this rending storm never even touched the outer coasts of this country, or raised anything worth calling a whisper about the continuity of our historic compromise. This is a historical fact, whether men rejoice in it or no; and a very remarkable and impressive fact too, when we come to consider it. But, though this is obvious, what may be called the converse is almost equally obvious. The world is coming to a conflict of extremes, and the popularity of King George had as little to do with the one sort of extreme as the other. The Republican had grown accustomed to a monarch; the Royalist had grown accustomed to a constitutional monarch; the monarch owed little to the new cult of monarchy. Continental States which have already been shaken by revolutions are under constant fear of being shaken again by restorations. But it is simply the fact touching ourselves, and our own unique insular tradition, that, when we have all said with deep and sincere sorrow, 'The King is dead,' not a soul thinks seriously of saying anything except 'Long live the King!'

The virtues of King George were rather specially of a

sort to correct the confusions and corruptions that have made modern government so insecure. What has most harmed modern government, including what we call representative government, is a certain quality that is seldom mentioned, though I think I have mentioned it, for I think it very serious. It is the loss of the old ideal which associated a love of liberty with a scorn of luxury. The first and best of the democratic idealists were always definite on this point. They demanded that a republican senator should show a republican simplicity. It was that which was to distinguish the senator from the courtier, and from the effeminacy of the Court. We have lived to see the Court set something of an example to the Senates. The King had considerably more republican simplicity, in that sense, than a good many republican plutocrats and millionaires. Nobody ever accused him of being a leader of the Smart Set, or of frequenting those bizarre night clubs where he might have found not a few of the popularly elected politicians. He had little appetite for luxury; he can hardly have had a very definite itch even for leisure. The declaration of abstinence which he made at the beginning of the War was very typical of him. It was not merely ritual or royal gesture; if he had been born in any other station there would have been something about him that was thus thrifty and vigilant and ready to renounce. And whether we agree or not with the theory of this or that renunciation, it is certain that this sort of thing was in trenchant contrast with the general use of social emancipation around him. There can be no doubt that it provided what has been very badly needed in our time, a sort of core of orderly and sensible living, in the very midst of a society which, like some pagan societies of the past, is in many ways not far from madness.

The popular suspicion which poisons so much of

popular government today is directly connected with the
exaggerated pursuit of pleasure. It is a suspicion, not only
of wealth, but of the waste of wealth. It is a suspicion
that almost anything may be a mere ladder to the life of
the rich, even an attack on the rich. A friend of mine
expressed it long ago, on the occasion of a political election, in lines which I hope are familiar—

> The evil power that buttressed privilege
> And went with women and champagne and bridge,
> Broke, and Democracy resumed her reign
> Which went with bridge and women and champagne.

Against this sort of impression, the whole attitude of the
late King was a very valuable corrective. It reminded us,
in a permanent personal manifestation, of the other and
better side of English administration; and especially of the
patience and loyalty of the public services, and of those
great permanent officials of whom he was the first. Upon
this side of public business and bureaucratic devotion
there is a general testimony to his thoroughness. I myself,
though not in the way of such things, have met many
men who were impressed by his knowledge of detail in
departments which they had imagined to be almost
private experiences of their own. He had certainly learned
much more, in all departments of life, than he ever presented as pretensions to the public; and in that sense it
might be said that his public life was only too private, and
had hardly enough of the old parade of popular
monarchy.

As a patriotic ruler and a public servant, especially in
the matter of responsibility and hard work, his reputation
was a thing universally assured. But as a private individual, I rather fancy that he was a good deal misunderstood. He had not, as his father had, the gesture

of public life, the presence that seems to fill platforms, the smile that includes crowds; and therefore he adopted in such things a less expansive dignity not without a touch of doggedness, and produced on some strangers an impression of being stolid. But, as a social personality, he was not stolid. Those who met him for the first time, with nothing but this previous impression of public occasions, were almost startled by his vivacity. He spoke frankly, sometimes very frankly, and did not disguise his healthy likes and dislikes. He was probably of the kind that would always prefer talking in private to speaking in public, but not because he had any inherent reluctance to speak. As is often the case with what would seem a mere popular sentiment, there was a certain instinctive accuracy about the phrase that called him the Sailor King. For his personality most immediately recalled a certain sort of lively though experienced naval officer; animated, anecdotal, fond of talking about important things in a casual way. Naturally, this aspect could not be known to most of us, except by accident or incidental privilege; but the indirect effects of it can be felt in innumerable stories even at second and third hand. If he was unfitted for the flamboyant kingcraft of Potsdam, he was the very reverse of a man who merely adopted the pose of the impenetrable, or tried to suggest significance by silence. He had views on a great variety of things, and did not hesitate to express them; only his self-expression was naturally conversational rather than oratorical. There is one thing, however, which is universally attested, both by the direct and the indirect impressions. He was quite unusually considerate; not only in the loose sense of being kindly, but in the literal sense of considering how to be kind. The strongest impressions of his thoughtfulness for others came from those who had been in the closest relation with him for many years, under conditions of Court life which generally breed an endless crop of complaints and rivalries and bitter recollections. 'Even in a palace life can be lived well,' said the emperor of the world; and in one or two cases, such as King George's, it can be added that it could hardly be lived anywhere more simply, or with less evil of pride.

ON LYING IN STATE

BEFORE the funeral of that good and faithful servant who had inherited the Crown of the Confessor and the Conqueror, the body lay in state, in the ceremonial phrase, in that most historical hall which the Conqueror's son had built, and in which an English King had once been tried for his life. The fact that the first King was murdered and the second executed, and this third King venerated as he actually was in death, may give cause for thought to those who simplify all history into a mere advancing antagonism against principalities and powers. But the ceremonial phrase itself is of some interest; precisely because such simplifiers would have called it 'merely' ceremonial. In recent times, especially at the end of the eighteenth century, when royal ritual and etiquette had piled up to the top of their complexity, as things always do before they crash, there was a widespread reaction against ceremonial; not merely among rationalists, but also among reasonable men. In that reaction the real meaning of such ceremonial was largely lost. Popular anger was aroused against those very pageants that had originally been instituted because they were popular.

This truth can be traced in the treatment, remote and recent and present, of the very phrase 'lying in state'. In the recent rationalistic interlude, now largely passing, the tendency was to insist with some irritation on the words 'in state'. The rational emancipators of humanity insisted that such pageantry was mere pomp; that such pomp was mere pomposity. The only defect of those admirable friends of humanity was that they knew no history. As a fact, the notion of a King lying in state was a part of the popular and not the pompous side of royalty. It was connected with the very ancient idea of the accessibility of the King; not on any later idea, even any new but necessary idea, of the privacy of the King. In the matter of a merely arrogant stateliness, the King was much less 'in state' when he showed himself to his people dead or alive, than when he did all his less recognized duties in dealing with State secrets. It meant that the mob might be excluded from the Council-Chamber; but it was admitted to the Death-Chamber.

To use an old phrase, such customs were founded upon the profound popular proverb that a cat may look at a king; not on any notion that a king would not look at a common man. That this was the historic truth, about the actual history of monarchy, good or bad, is proved by all the other facts of the case. When kingship had risen to its most extraordinary and even exaggerated eminence, as in the great France of the *Grand Siècle,* people were admitted, not merely to the death-chamber when the King was dead, but to the bed-chamber when he was alive. Crowds poured through the dressing-room of Louis XIV, that almost almighty monarch, and saw him washing and dressing and even drinking emetics. He could be an autocrat, a conqueror, a controller of parliaments; he could be everything but a private person. Buried deep, in the very depths of this singular human institution, was the idea that the people possessed their monarch, like a public monument, or even a public park. He ruled them, but they owned him.

That this popular vision of the Monarch had grown out of proportion by the time of the *Roi Soleil,* is probably proved by the reaction that followed soon after; the reaction that we call the Revolution. But it had been primarily a popular idea. In fact, it was perhaps more purely popular than most, or many of the best, of the Revolutionists, who were often aristocrats and generally intellectuals. Anyhow, we can see it forming far back in medieval times; and it is always concerned with this almost sacramental conception of access to the body of the King. In the wildest wars of the feudal times, in France and England, and especially in Scotland, we find factions attaching enormous importance to the mere material fact of having the King among them; even as a child or a captive or an imbecile. They carried the King about with them, as if he were a sort of sacred relic or fetish or mascot; and they seem to have felt that the presence even of reluctant royalty gave them an advantage over their rivals. And the reason was, fundamentally, that the King was always popular; as no feudal lord was popular. That submerged instinct of history, which exists in the ignorant in the form of tradition, and is often much truer than history, remembered something that the most wicked kings could not entirely destroy; that far back in the foundations of Christendom, saints and missionaries of the old civilization had dedicated this man to be the father of the people. There had never been any such definite dedication of any mere feudal fighter or raider. He was *Dominus Rex,* and different from other men; even if he were a tyrant. It has been truly remarked that no medieval Regent was ever a success. King John is our own typical tyrant; but it is only fair to him to remember that he had been a Regent. And in those remote times of the roots of national or modern monarchy, there is perpetually the emphasis upon the bodily presence of the responsible prince. It was so strong that it extended to the idea of a body even when it was only a body.

It is perhaps a deep criticism of the modern mind that

we have fallen into the habit of only talking about a body when we mean a corpse. Even the old phrase *Habeas Corpus,* as well as older and more sacred and sacramental phrases, recalls a world of feeling in which a living body was also described as a body. But in any case, this old mystical tradition extended from the living body to the dead. As the companions of the Cid brought out even his dead body in battle-armour and on horse-back, that it might be an ensign for the Christians and a trumpet of defiance against the Moors, so the old traditional feeling of the royal presence always extended to the presence of death. It always had this character of a direct popular appeal. Sometimes, for various reasons, it was used for a political appeal. The old Kings were sometimes shown with their faces uncovered; in some cases, for a practical proclamation to the crowd; as, for instance, to show that the King was really dead. But always the idea of a crowd passing before his coffin, when he was dead, was part of the same idea as the right of personally offering petitions when he was alive. It was the idea that the palace was not merely a private house; that it was, in fact, the public's house. It was a house where the doors stood open. The people owned the King.

THE ALPHABET OF GIANTS

In one sense the most impressive building at Wembley Exhibition was probably the Queen's Dolls-House. The sense in which I say this refers to the value of small models of big things. It seems to me that man has made things almost too great for his own imagination to measure. He is too much at home in his house, and sometimes he cannot see the city any more than he can see the earth. It may be easier to use the copy rather than the real thing as a working model for real education. For about the remains or ruins of the great art of building there is a curious paradox of popular misconception, which is not easy to describe.

Architecture is the alphabet of giants; it is the largest system of symbols ever made to meet the eyes of men. A tower stands up like a sort of simplified statue, of much more than 'heroic size'. A façade is rightly called a face; it has something of the character of a huge human face fading or simplifying itself into the formality of a diagram; we see it in the childish sketches of a cottage with windows for eyes and the front-door for a mouth. We feel as if architecture were a simplified art of statuary and portraiture, just as the statuary and portraiture of ancient Egypt or Nineveh really were simplified and stiffened almost to the severity of architecture. It is as if a monolith were a headless body, or a dome were a hairless skull. Seen for a moment in this light, or this twilight, all architecture takes on mysterious lines of life and a movement as of signals. Nor is this merely fanciful, for it inheres in much of our habitual language on the subject. We say that a spire points to the sky, as if it really lifted a finger. We say that windows look over a landscape, as if windows were really eyes.

There is, then, a universal instinct that architecture has something to say; that it is, as it were, trying to say it. Some aesthetes still maintain that art is unmoral—or, in effect, that it is unmeaning. But they ought really to be pursuing the opposite line of progress and finding more meanings instead of less. Instead of treating religious pictures as decorative patterns, they would have much better fun proving that even patterns are religious. They would have much better fun looking for their religion in the wallpaper or the Turkey carpet. But this is a digression. The point is that architecture also, like the more obvious arts of representation, has about it something that suggests a proclamation or a message; but that its speciality is the size or scale upon which the message can be given. The message is given on a megaphone; the proclamation is distributed by a loudspeaker. The size of a building is the most obvious thing to say about it; it is meant to be the most obvious thing to see in it. Mere size is meant to be self-evident and therefore simple; a colossal commonplace. Yet, strangely enough, while this art presents its symbols on a vast scale, and staring at the sun, they remain in many ways more elusive and delicate than a drawing in silverpoint or a light tracery in lace. The hieroglyphs are as huge as Assyrian bulls; but they are not hieroglyphs that everybody can read. Strangely enough, they are not only things that few can read, they are sometimes things that few can see. It would almost seem that they are too large to be seen.

It is certainly strange that the historical lessons of architecture have not always been easily understood. Things have been dismissed as trifles when the very litter

and leavings of them were terrific. Things have been neglected as naked or barbarous when the smallest scrap of
them was complex and ornate. Civilizations have been
loosely lumped together when the very skyline of their
cities wrote the difference upon the sky. The vulgar
example, a very vulgar example, is that of the insular
English gentleman or still more frequently, I grieve to
say, the insular English lady—who travels in India without any idea about the Indian races and religions, except
that they are all one dim mob to be described as 'natives'.
Yet one would fancy, for instance, that the difference
between the Moslem and the Brahmin tradition was
something almost as obvious to the eye as the difference
between a wigwam and a Wimbledon villa. The one
tradition prides itself on carrying through a scheme of
the most colossal scale while remaining almost appallingly
impersonal. All that ornament may be literally called
featureless in the sense of faceless; it must contain no
portraiture of man or beast or bird. We are not to look
for it any more than for a human figure in the most complicated figures of Euclid. This element is emphasized
wherever the Moslem creed is most emphatic. Round the
great Mosque of Omar in Jerusalem the most apparently
florid decoration consists only of handwriting, of elaborate Arabic script, defining the unity of God. The heraldic
symbol of the Caliphate does not rival the eagle of Rome
or the lion of England, or even the lilies of France, except
with the cold horns of the hollow moon.

It is this austerity that makes a miracle even of Moslem
luxury. The magnificence of a thing like the Taj Mahal
is increased by a great abnegation. The other Eastern
tradition is at the very opposite extreme. It boils, one
might say it bubbles, with bodily representations. There
are patterns made out of swaying figures with monstrous

hips. There are gods many-headed as if everything were doubling and trebling; gods who wave wild arms to us like the numberless arms of a forest. Some have represented Asia as a nightmare of the over-population of the earth; and it would seem as if the very heavens were over-populated. Taken by itself, this would be a superficial view of Indian polytheism. But the point is that the super-cilious tourist could not see even the startling contrast between the iconoclast and the idolater. Therefore, he could never see the really reconciling truth about Islam— that it was much more of a war against the gods of Asia than against the God of Christendom.

It is hardly surprising that the superior person could learn no history from the architecture of Asia, for he could not learn it from the architecture of England. From the Renaissance to the Ruskinian epoch he went on talking of the Middle Ages as merely benighted and barbaric. Yet in every other English village a colossal contrast contradicted him flatly. A great medieval build-ing stood up among the more modern buildings like a mountain among molehills. It stood up like a mountain; but people could not see it. They still went on saying that tumbledown cottages had been made in an age of pro-gress and the eternal tower had been made in an age of ignorance. Perhaps that also was too large to be seen; and perhaps that also might be seen better in a smaller space or on a smaller model. But for that we must wait for another exhibition—not of the Empire, but of the English story; and perhaps it may be even more enlightening.

BAROQUE AND GOTHIC
ARCHITECTURE

Much has been written recently about a revival of interest in what is called the Baroque—the rather riotous sort of Renaissance architecture which broke out all over Europe, largely in connexion with the Counter-Reformation and largely leading up to what the French call the Great Century, the noontide glory of the *Roi Soleil*. Critics are saying, with some justice, that the very medievalists who rightly condemned the reckless Renaissance contempt for the Gothic have since exhibited a quite equally reckless contempt for all the results of the Renaissance. As the one was called Gothic merely in the sense of the barbaric, so the other is called Rococo merely in the sense of florid or absurd. The classical foundations of Rome are not necessarily bad because the pointed shrines in Normandy are good; and if it is hard to imagine how anyone ever thought that a savage had designed St Ouen's, we have even more detailed evidence that it was not exactly a fool who designed St Peter's.

We all have our preferences, we all probably have our prejudices about these things; but even medievalists like myself may well admit that some of us have shown prejudice as well as preference. We may well admit that, even when we are illuminated with all the windows of Chartres, even when we are rejoicing in some glorious Gothic lantern of flamboyant glass, we are in a sense living in glass houses and should not throw stones. Certainly we should not cast the first stone at every stonemason who does not happen to be a medieval stone-

mason. To take that position is to be every bit as ignorant
and stupid as those great Renaissance classicists who
thought themselves so enlightened and so wise. Certainly
they were Vandals when they thought they were attack-
ing Goths. But the Gothicists are really Goths when they
march only to sack the temples of Rome.

So much even a man of medieval sympathies may well
concede to those who condemn anything as Pagan if it
is not Pugin. But we will probably add that the worst
weakness of the medievalists is that they fall short of the
medievals. The real trouble has been that even those who
admired Gothic most could not revive the part of it that
was most admirable. The most wonderful thing about
Gothic was the spontaneous individual craftsmanship,
especially in its sanctification of the grotesque. But there
was nothing specially spontaneous, there was nothing
specially individual, there was certainly nothing specially
grotesque, about the pallid and pointed church architecture that began with the Victorian High Churchman
and is now the pattern of every Wesleyan or Congrega-
tionalist chapel in Surbiton or Streatham. The worthy
Wesleyan would be gravely surprised if he saw his pew
decorated with some of the carvings found on the
Miserere seats of the monks. The speculative builder in
Surbiton would be distinctly pained if he found an
ordinary bricklayer chipping a brick about to make a
hideous face, certainly to suit the fancy of the labourer,
and possibly to be a caricature of the foreman.

This sort of variety within a framework of unity was
the real merit of the medieval world, and it is nearly
impossible in the modern world. Anyhow, it is quite as
impossible in the Gothic chapel in Streatham as it is in
the classical temple in Rome. That is what I mean by
saying that the modern stained glass attitudinizer is

living in a glass house or is open to a *tu quoque*; he is not really carving his own gargoyles any more than the classicist, and anybody who dared to cast a real stone devil among us might be killing two birds with one stone. He might be not only rebuking classicism for not being Gothic, but even more sharply rebuking Gothic for not being Gothic. In other words, the real objection to revivals of medievalism is that they are not medieval enough.

The Baroque in art and architecture, however, had its own sort of freedom and fantasy; and, as it was produced under social conditions more like our own, it is natural that some of us should turn to it with a new understanding and sympathy. Nevertheless, the understanding and sympathy are quite new, and that for a reason that is rather interesting in itself. It arises from the fact that the full civilization in which this expanded and even extravagant form of classicism flourished is one from which we in England have been cut off by a curious historical accident. The period which was most positive in French history was curiously negative in English history. It is like the case of one of those florid classical masks so often seen in the sculpture and decoration of the Baroque period. Only the French beheld it solid and in the round; a full and featured face; the noble mask of Comedy or of Tragedy; for the smile was the smile of Molière and the frown was the frown of Racine. But we were on the concave and not the convex side of that mould or protuberance. At that particular period, we saw it as something hollow and empty; even when we imitated it, we used it as a mask and hardly saw it as a face.

Indeed, we imitated the French without admiring them—or, at any rate, we admired them without praising them. They were at once our enemies and our models; but that very fact shows that they were at that moment at their best and we almost at our worst. Wycherley wrote an English version of the noblest of all the plays of Molière, and it is pretty ignoble. It is almost enough to ask where Molière has stood among French writers and where Wycherley has stood among English. Anyhow, it will be agreed that our great period was rather the age of Shakespeare than the age of Wycherley. The reasons for this contrast are probably political and may be very roughly suggested by saying that the natural outcome and climax of the Renaissance, good or bad, was the thing which Charles I failed in achieving and which Henry VIII only seemed to achieve. It was the replacing of a strong Church by a strong State and even by a strong King.

In France this strong State was established, with such advantages as that conception has, in all sorts of things down to the leadership of fashion and the patronage of art and architecture. In England it was thwarted and broken up, for good or evil, by factions, and especially by the faction of the Whig aristocrats. Therefore, if we want to judge that strong State which was the spirit of the time, and balance its good and evil, England happens to be a very unfortunate corner of Europe in which to study it. The English Puritans had their own virtues; the English Whigs had their own case; but they do not tell us much of what was happening in the world just then, or of that positive and constructive culture whose architectural symbol was the Baroque.

It seems to me very odd that internationalists, who rebuke the narrowness of national things, seldom sympathize with really international things. Thus the man who is always hoping that a Europe without flags or frontiers will exist in the future, is quite annoyed to discover that a Europe without flags or frontiers really existed in the past. He wants to get nearer to a World State and he hates the nearest that the world ever came to a World State—the Roman Empire. I find the most enlightened Englishmen strangely blind to the positive European importance of the Grand Siècle. They seem to be as jealous of Louis XIV as if he were still alive. But a good historian will feel something of the magnificence of the legend of Louis, just as he will feel something of the magnificence of the legend of Elizabeth. You cannot understand France without one, or England without the other—or Europe without both.

ROBERT BRUCE AND HIS AGE

In 1314, on the Vigil of John the Baptist, a long and
magnificent war-array under the banner of the great
Plantagenets, and of an epoch when chivalry was already
a pageant, came rolling out of the south over the lowlands
that lie around the crag and castle of Stirling. They
reached a small and marshy brook called the Bannock,
behind which were posted forces of uncertain but certainly far inferior numbers, clumps of spearmen, mainly
infantry, under the command of a tall gentleman of
Norman extraction whom many regarded as an adven-
turer. There was an unconscious creative quality in him
and a simplicity in good and evil which is almost incom-
prehensible to those who have not the key of that older
Christendom. He had become a sincere patriot by
accident or (one might almost say) by mistake. He became an excellent King by something like usurpation.
He was probably prouder of his strong body than of his
very strong brain. Murder and sacrilege and all sorts of
indefensible things had brought him at last to the defence
of his country—or, if you will, to the creation of it. The
great host swept on and struck the smaller one here
and there, but unsuccessfully; it was entangled in rude
man-traps and muddy river banks and hung there, fighting heavily; and on the second day it broke.

There are three stages through which the mind of a
modern man should pass in connexion with what may
be called the romance of the Middle Ages. The Middle
Ages were, in some ways, romantic. The Scots are wildly
romantic. And the purely romantic aspect of the period

has been excellently symbolized in the cult of Bannock-burn. There are all the romantic ingredients—the triumph against odds, the defence of the soil, and above all, the bodily peril of the prince and leader. Yet even the Scots are not always romantic; nor were the Middle Ages. I repeat, therefore, that there are three stages through which a thinking man goes in his consideration of such a romance as that of Robert Bruce, 'the third best knight in Christendom'. They say that second thoughts are best, but I incline to disagree. I think that third thoughts are sometimes best. But I think that first thoughts are much better than second thoughts, and have more resemblance to the real ripeness of third thoughts. In the first stage we act merely on instinct; and are sometimes right. In the second stage we act merely on reason, and are fairly frequently wrong. In the third and truly reasonable stage we use our reason until we understand our instincts. And if we do that with romance we shall come pretty near reality.

The first stage might be symbolized in Miss Jane Porter's 'Scottish Chiefs', in which, as Thackeray said, William Wallace goes into battle with a tear in his eye and a cambric handkerchief in his hand. In other words, it is a romance of no particular age or country, but certainly more modern than medieval; and with no complexity of human nature, but only a war between heroes and villains. It is in this stage that boys die daily for Mary Queen of Scots, or girls make short work of the constitutional complications that enmeshed Charles I. But in so far as the feeling is idealistic, it really is medieval; and, what is much more important, right. And just as it associated loyalty with the House of Stuart, it associated liberty with the House of Bruce. Bruce drew the sword for Scottish freedom, and there is an end of it.

It is true that most of those young people would be puzzled to define the position either of freedom or Scotland in connexion with the controversy about the Suzerainty. But all the same the young people are right, much more right than they are when they learn a little more.

The second stage begins about the time that we begin to read Carlyle and Kingsley. We learn that the great men of the Middle Ages were not waxwork heroes, but statesmen, and even diplomatists; that the wicked things they did were designed to great ends of policy and dominion. In this intellectual phase, and especially under these intellectual influences, it is common to consider the consolidation of great States, the spreading of unified systems, as the great triumph in politics. In this stage, therefore, it is common to regret the death of Edward I and the failure of Edward II; and to regard Bruce somewhat as a sentimental obstacle. It leads sometimes to that excusing of tyranny which is the weakest tendency in human nature. It even leads sometimes to maintaining that all wars were fought for economic and industrial reasons; but into that mire of mental decay we need not follow it. But certainly, if I have to choose between Miss Jane Porter and such historical philosophers as Carlyle and Froude, I am for Miss Jane Porter. Bring me my claymore—and my cambric handkerchief. Miss Porter may have been ignorant of the cruelties alleged against Wallace in his Northumbrian raid, or she may not have believed in them. But she would never have excused, still less admired them, as Froude does the cruelties of the Tudors. Nor would Wallace himself have admired them, even if he'd done them. Miss Jane Porter is more manly than Froude.

At the third stage the student, if he is lucky enough

to get so far, comes to a view much more subtle and experienced than the first, but one by which he sees that the first had a great deal in it after all. He has learned that all men are mean, but especially great men. He knows that no valour and inspiration can save a man from the rebuke of Nathan; that no faith and holiness can insure him against the crowing of the cock. He knows that the best you can say of any man is to compare him to the curate's egg. But though he will know that only parts of Bruce and Wallace were heroic, he will also know that such parts as were heroic were more akin to the hero-worship of 'Frederick the Great'. Whatever the real knight held in his hand (a letter to a money-lender, as like as not), the ideal knight did hold the handkerchief of sensibility. And the student will conclude, though not with the old cut-and-dried conclusion, that there really was a meaning in fighting for the freedom of Scotland.

This second reversal of the vision generally comes if or when the student takes the startling course of reading what was written about medieval characters by the people who knew them. If Miss Porter's book stands for the first stage and Carlyle's essays for the second, the third begins with any three lines of any original chronicle or charter really written in the fourteenth century. The impression is indescribable, but it is instantaneous. The spirit that loathes the past as savage and inhuman, the much viler spirit that actually *admires* it as savage and inhuman, will not survive the reading of three average pages that were written when that past was present. Cruelties can be found in page after page; but cruelties of human reaction and complex legality and tangled retaliation; but never indifference to kindness. There are other indescribable things, the much stronger presence and bustle of the populace in the picture than the modern reader expects; and all the popular things being specially soaked in religion. If a superstition means something superimposed on people, medieval religion was the opposite of superstitious. You might as well say farmers' apples were superimposed on boys; it was the adventure of their lives. They are always trying to get back to the subject even when they are supposed to be talking about something else—say Bannockburn.

But there is another impression which grows more slowly, but more surely, from even a very few seeds of fact, for I do not claim any but a fragmentary reading of the records. And that is the impression that what the struggling and mysterious Middle Ages were getting at was, first and last, Freedom. But they attempted freedom always through division and definition, rights and privileges, orders, guilds, colleges—among other things, nations. For the nations did emerge. The Imperialism that tried to hold half Europe did break up before more independent—or, if you will, more jealous—loyalties. And some of the thanks we give to the great heart that fell in ashes at Rouen. I will not withhold from that much faultier heart that Douglas flung among the Moors.

WHAT MIGHT HAVE BEEN

THE test of a man's culture and liberality is his attitude towards the things that never happened. The test of historians especially, and of their possession of the true historical spirit, is the depth of their absorption, and the vividness of their vision, of the things that never happened. It is the things that never happened which enlarge the mind. Nobody who understands them can be narrow. Some of the historians have never heard of what never happened. In their case the test has been decisive indeed.

By the things that never happened, I mean the things that nearly happened. I do not mean fables or romances or legends that are obviously legendary. I mean the things that might have been, but which for some reason could not be. I mean the *alternative* history of England or France or Rome. Now the provincial person, even when he is a provincial professor, lives in a prison of what really happened. He may be prodigiously learned about what really happened; but because of his dense and disgusting ignorance on the subject of what never happened, he is doomed always to be as limited as he is learned. Certain things having taken place, he cannot unthink them, or get behind them, or escape from them into the wider possibilities of the world. For instance, if he is an Englishman he is quite right to be an English patriot; for loyalty and affection naturally belong to the department of the thing that really exists. But the English professor is often much more than an English patriot. The English professor is an English prisoner; the walls of the national castle, when once it has been built, shut off from him altogether the wide plains of the world, in which other things might have been built.

Thus we hear a great deal of discussion for and against the Middle Ages. One fact, which is not especially for or against, must surely be obvious to anybody who knows anything at all about the Middle Ages. And that is that one of the things that nearly happened was a single, solid United Kingdom of Anglo-France. From the time when the first Norman soldier disembarked before Hastings, to the time when the last English soldier marched out of Calais, it appeared a perfectly natural thing to thousands of people that the two nations might be one nation. At this moment the two nations are rather less like one nation than any two nations of the world. Most English internationalists seem to interpret universal brotherhood as the duty of loving Humanity and hating France. I, not being an English internationalist (thank God), am very fond of France and the French. I am capable of loving foreigners; but I love the French as the most foreign of all foreigners. The sharp and abrupt difference between the English and the French is rather more obvious to those who really love the French than to those who only stupidly hate them.

The educated English all talked and thought in French almost down to the time of Agincourt; and even after Agincourt whole sections of the French supported the attempt of the English to unite the two crowns by conquest. The other spirit was already in the field, and I doubt not it was the better spirit; the spirit of St Joan that was like a flaming sword; the sword of an angel but a sword that smote asunder. I, for one, am national and rejoice that the nations were born. But a man is not merely national, but also narrow, if he cannot realize that something larger and more imperial might have been born; a great Western State that would have been no more French than English, and no more English than French. It might have made all sorts of extraordinary differences to the subsequent story of mankind; and heaven knows what would have happened to the Puritans and the French Revolution and the British Empire, and all sorts of things to which we pay such solemn respect merely because they have managed to happen. It is a good thing, every now and then, to turn from them and listen to the fascinating and thrilling story of the things that did not happen.

Of course one could give any number of other examples. But it is my whole point here to avoid hackneyed examples. I am dealing with the things the provincial person has not thought of. It is easy enough to ask what would have happened if Waterloo had gone the other way; it is easy to ask because it is idle to answer. It would not have made much difference if Waterloo had gone the other way. Napoleon had not enough forces, anyhow, to crush all that was now on the march against him. But it would be interesting to ask what would have happened if Wattignies had gone the other way. And that is why the ordinary Englishman who speculates about Waterloo has hardly ever heard of Wattignies.

Now these speculations affect one aspect of a current controversy: the perpetual debate in the newspapers about Progress and Decadence or the Decline of the West. One class of popular writers are perpetually telling us that the world has always been growing better and better; others, rather less popular, that it has for some time been growing steadily worse. Personally, I cannot understand anybody thinking it has ever grown *steadily* anything. If Humanism was an advance, I cannot see how Calvinism can have been an advance on that advance. If the crowds rushing to the Amphitheatre were rushing in the right direction, the hermits rushing to the desert cannot have been rushing in the same direction. But, anyhow, in this dispute, the disputants generally compare some old cause with some new cause, or some hypothetical good old times with some equally hypothetical good new times. But the general impression which history produces on my own mind is neither of these. In most cases, it seems to me, the right thing was not the thing that ruled and not the thing that rebelled, but a third thing that was never quite strong enough either to rebel or rule. The thing that haunts the historical imagination most, I think, is not Atlantis or Utopia, not the Golden Age or the New Jerusalem, not the Good Old Days or the Good Time Coming, but the gold that men missed or rejected and the good time that might have come.

Whether or no the world is travelling towards the right goal, it seems to me to have almost invariably taken the wrong turning. Whether or no it is now rather nearer to it, I am sure it has come nearer by a vast needless détour, and missed any number of short cuts that were much nearer. I doubt if any thinking person, of any belief or unbelief, does not wish in his heart that the end of medievalism had meant the triumph of the Humanists like Erasmus and More, rather than of the rabid Puritans like Calvin and Knox. Indeed, the name of Thomas More is not inappropriate here, for more reasons than one. It was he who invented the very word Utopia; and then, finding the changes he saw so different from the changes he desired, would not have the book translated into English. Utopia is not at the beginning of the world or the end of the world. Utopia has been something always near and never discovered.

THE AGE OF REASON

I

THE eighteenth century is an excellent illustration of a false historical fashion. It is the fashion of abusing a thing, first for one obvious reason, then for another quite opposite reason; and then leaving it alone with all its incompatible vices unreconciled and unexplained. Anyone can describe that age as the age of powder and patches and high-heeled shoes and elaborate bows and mincing compliments. Anybody can describe it as the age of bludgeons and bloody noses and black patches over the eye, as in the pictures of Hogarth; of dirt and drunkenness and brutal sports. As details, they are both true; as generalizations, they cannot be both true. As philosophical explanations, they cannot come within a thousand miles of being true. As explanations, they cannot explain anything; for they cannot explain each other.

We may call eighteenth-century people's dressing and barbering and behaviour artificial, but that gets us no nearer to explaining why we have to complain of them the next moment for being a great deal too natural. For they were virile to the point of violence and anarchy. If it was the age of wigs, it was also the age of wigs on the green. It was not only concerned with the nice conduct of a clouded cane, but often with the nasty conduct of a loaded cudgel. If we only want to make a case against the eighteenth century, we can throw all these ill-matched things at it and leave them there in a heap. But that does not explain anything; not even our own antagonism or our own action.

I have had to deal with a similar fallacy in relation to religious history. I have pointed out that the people who only wanted to make a case against Christianity or the Middle Ages, or what not, were content simply to say that monks were too meek and Crusaders too fierce, and feudalism too crude and heraldry too complicated. In other words, they blamed the age for being as mild as the Confessor and as violent as Coeur de Lion, but they gave no reason for the same thing being two opposite things at once. Many of them, in criticizing what I said, have thought it quite enough to say that the two statements were quite true; and this in itself is also quite true. But you have not understood the thing until you have understood its contradiction; until (especially) you understand even its misunderstanding.

The only way to understand an age, whether it be the Age of Reason or the Age of Faith, is to get behind these mere criminal charges, which are used to support each other and really destroy each other. It is to find some common spirit that can be polished in that particular way and coarse in that particular way. A mystical conviction is the cause both of the Franciscan being friendly and the Crusader being hostile. A rational conviction is the cause both of Dr Johnson being ceremonious and Dr Johnson being rude. But it is necessary to realize something of what that rational conviction really was; and the only spirit in which it is worth while to study history is the spirit which can feel a certain enthusiasm for the ideal of each time in turn.

The eighteenth century itself is not a century, as centuries go, that is specially attractive to me. There were not enough fairy-tales in it for my taste; certainly there were not anything like so many people believing in fairies then as there are now. It had no great understanding

of children. The men of that time had forgotten the
Holy Child of medieval times and had not yet heard of
the Happy Child of modern literature. They could not
imagine a Peter Pan, for they had lost the religious
traditions both of Pan and of Peter. They had silenced
all those subconscious voices which speak to simple people
of the wonders hidden in this world. In short, they were
ignorant of all the thousand things that only the ignorant
ever know.

But though I should not be individually drawn towards the Age of Reason as compared with many ages
I think really much more reasonable, if I had to deal
with that age I should deal with it more reasonably. I
should not criticize it as its own rationalistic critics do.
I should not pick out things here and there that happened to offend our modern taste, though in totally
opposite ways. I should not blame Chesterfield for being foppish and Johnson for being slovenly; call a minuet
stilted and a cockfight vulgar; and then heave a sigh and
thank God that I live in better days. That is the way in
which the stupidest sort of tourist criticizes a foreign
country; he thinks everything is being done badly, because he has never tried to find out what people are trying
to do.

I should begin at the other end and try to find out
what the eighteenth century was trying to do. I should
ask what spirit really prompted their more spirited efforts.
The true historian does *not* want to be told the realities
of the eighteenth century; that is, that they had stuffier
bedrooms or stuffier cravats. The true historian wants to
be told the ideal of the eighteenth century; the things
that a man dreamed of in his stuffy bedroom or thought
about when he had forgotten his stock. The mere facts
about their vesture or ventilation are not really facts

about them; they are rather facts about us. They are the things that *we* notice, because to us they are new even in being old. It may throw some light on *our* character or conditions that this or that detail stands out in a startling fashion from the other details. But it does not throw much light on the minds of our ancestors. The really valuable sort of historical imagination is to guess the things they were thinking about.

The religion of the eighteenth century was finely expressed in the motto of a group of Scottish debating societies famous as the Associated Societies of Edinburgh University. It was *Gloria hominis ratio et oratio* : the glory of man is reason and speech. Their ideal was public spirit in the true sense of the publishing of things; the power of declaring aloud in the forum the secrets of the palace or the corruptions of the senate. There were secrets and corruptions enough, of course, as there are in all times; not so many, I think, as there are in our own time. But this was the vision, the ambition, the day-dream. This was what an honest man wanted to be and a dishonest man pretended to be. The ideal type of that time was what Walpole called a Boy; what the Boy called a Patriot. He was to be a lucid orator denouncing courtiers and placemen; a tribune. He can only be under-stood in the light of that great Latin literature which these men loved and studied.

We sneer at the old gentlemen quoting Horace while hobnobbing over their port; as if they only quoted Horace when he was hobnobbing over his Falernian. We forget that quoting Horace meant more often quot-ing great lines about Regulus defying torture for the Republic or the poet returning to the temples of the gods of Rome. Judged by its own moral ideal, which is the only just judgement, the eighteenth century was not so

I

bad as we make out; possibly was not so bad as we are. We talk of its political corruption, but we talk of it because it was talked about. It was exposed and even punished. Great men like Marlborough, powerful men like Dundas, were really forced to resign; often even forced to disgorge. They were much less completely protected than corrupt politicians in our own time; and it is no very satisfactory proof of their artificiality and our realism that they powdered heads while we whitewash reputations.

II

It seems to me that it would be an extraordinarily interesting study of the mind of the eighteenth century to picture what that mind would really expect to see in the twentieth. There would be something very subtle in the comedy of a gentleman of the eighteenth century dealing with ladies of the twentieth century. It would be curious to note how he would be in some ways more coarse and in some ways more polished. He would probably be plainer in his speech, but more ceremonious in his movements. He would say things to the lady while bowing over her hand which the most sprightly hero of our recent fiction would hardly say to her while sitting on her head. When Marie Antoinette and her courtiers posed in the manner of the shepherds of Watteau, they were already talking about the dawn of a more enlightened and liberal age, and may well have wondered about the world in the twentieth century. When Hogarth was drawing some satiric series like the Stages of Cruelty, he may well have wondered whether the world would still be as barbarous in the twentieth century, or whether by that time reason and philanthropy would have prevailed. Naturally it would depend a great deal on the sort of

individual who was precipitated from their age to ours;
there were doubtless many commonplace cock-fighting
squires who knew as little about the future then as our
earnest social prophets know now. But there were already
in the eighteenth century some idealists who would have
been delighted to see the future triumph of humanity.
They would also be a good deal disappointed if they
saw it.

What is really interesting about the Age of Reason is
that the political economists and practical reformers
would every one of them believe what nobody now be-
lieves at all. They would not only have believed, most
probably, that England would be more prosperous, more
happy, and more equal in the twentieth century than in
the eighteenth or nineteenth. They would also have believed that it would become more prosperous, free, and
equal *through* commercial competition, *through* scientific selfishness, *through* the removal of all restrictions on
trading, talking, or anything else. Nothing would have
surprised a man like Bentham or a man like Godwin
more completely than the discovery that Liberty or
Laissez Faire had not made a huge addition to human
happiness by the beginning of the twentieth century.
As a matter of fact, as applied, they have made a huge
addition to human muddle and misery, and taken us
round by a long detour (and a very dusty road) back to
very much where we were before. We have to consider
anew the nature of Liberty and its relation to Govern-
ments. In that sense we are all of us really back in the
eighteenth century.

III

Unless I am much mistaken, modern people are going
to have a reaction against democracy before they have

tried it. We are always being told that the present system in highly organized industrial states is democracy; and that being so, it is hardly to be wondered at that democracy has become unpopular. But it is not really true that popular government has become unpopular. It is rather that people have ceased to think that in either sense our government is popular. The truth is that those who developed the democratic doctrine in modern times did not intend it for anything at all resembling the modern world, perhaps the most ancient of all possible worlds. They thought of the agricultural commonwealths of antiquity, and went back past even the Roman Empire to find the Roman Republic. But Rome was a republic when Rome was a village. Those eighteenth-century idealists often actually lived in villages; always in countries that were dotted with villages. They did not know what sort of a world of steam and steel their descendants were going to inherit. The French Revolution came before the Industrial Revolution. They were perpetually talking about the citizen, but they thought of him as a citizen and not merely as something in the city. They certainly had no conception of the colossal and complicated thing that we now mean by a city.

It is highly characteristic of the tone of the eighteenth century that they generally talked of London as 'the town'. They said : 'All the town is talking about my Lord Banglebury's duel with Mr Pickles.' In the sound and sense of the word there was something compact and comfortable; as of a world still small enough to know itself, like a village. When these people talked about democracy they did indeed mean the government of the people, by the people, for the people. But they meant the government of people they knew, by people they knew, for people they knew. They meant the government of people who knew each other, by people who knew each other, for people who knew each other. I think it highly doubtful whether any of the eighteenth-century democratic theorists, whether Payne or Jefferson or Condorcet, would have expected a vast and vague society like ours to be a democracy. I think they would have thought it, however reluctantly, a case for Caesar and the *panem et circenses*. But it is not, of course, merely the material side of society that has upset such calculations. It is much more the moral factor; which is also, in every sense, alas! a very material factor. It is what the scientific, or those who think themselves scientific, always call the economic factor. It can be expressed better in one word; and that word is not democracy but plutocracy.

It must always be remembered that the scale of financial action was then smaller even for the rich. The Court of Versailles did not handle such sums as any stockjobber will now waste on a week's luxury. Kings and queens were richer relatively and not positively. And the size of economic operations today is a new and abnormal power in the history of the world. It covers much more of the surface of the world. It is international where the old luxury was almost local. But this vulgar and sprawling plutocracy does not deserve to be called a democracy, even by one who uses it as a term of abuse. The old classic spirit of democracy is much more present in the independent citizen who is ready to resist it, who in this respect is much more like the Stoic and Tribune admired by the Fathers of the Republic.

THE VICTORIANS

I HAVE been wandering about in the South of France, reading hardly anything except French newspapers; which, by the way, are almost invariably worth reading. It is doubtless a Latin eccentricity; but they attach more importance to how a thing is written than to how it is printed. But everyone will understand, and certainly the French themselves would be the first to understand, that anything coming to such a wanderer, however indirectly, from his own country has an instant and imperious challenge to the emotions, which mere internationalism can never destroy or even define. And I found in a remote hotel, with a reaction amounting to tears, an ancient copy of a very modern London weekly paper, largely devoted to literary reviews; and raising a question for which I am always seeking the answer. I have no idea how old the issue was; but it was certainly subsequent to Queen Victoria's Coronation, and even to her death; because a prominent feature was a review on a book about 'The Victorians'. And naturally we never called ourselves Victorians while we really were Victorians. On the other hand, since I neglected to note the date, it may really have been a quite recent date; and the book in question may be the very latest work on the subject. At least it may be the latest; but I rather doubt whether it will be the last. For the Victorians, whatever else they were, were people whom the new generation may have managed to despise, but have certainly never managed to dismiss. The same age which boasts of having broken away finally from Victorianism is the age which it seems impossible to restrain from writing plays about Browning, books about Brontës, lives of such very limited and localized Victorians as Palmerston and Disraeli; and, above all, a permanent Victorian torrent of books about Queen Victoria herself. In the days dismissed as Victorian, nobody could ever have dreamed that Prince Albert would ever become so important an historical figure again. Look up the early volumes of *Punch,* and see what the writers made of the Prince Consort then; and you will hardly find it credible to read what Miss Sitwell, or Mr Laurence Housman, or even the late Lytton Strachey, have made of him now.

That is perhaps the first and queerest thing about the present phase. It set out avowedly to be anti-Victorian, and on many points it has become more Victorian than the Victorians. Of course the arbitrary title covers such a vast variety of names and types and tendencies, that it may be said that it is futile in any case to treat it as a whole; but I think myself that in this respect there is more intelligence in the instinct both of its antagonists and its admirers. I fancy that there really was something human and historic that can really be called Victorianism; though it is very difficult to define rightly; and almost invariably defined wrongly. Certainly, in the mere modern impatience which calls it stale and stuffy, it is defined utterly wrongly. There is a wonderfully widespread impression that the Victorian Age was very solid or stolid; either in virtue or else in hypocrisy. This is, especially over the great part of the period, quite surprisingly untrue. Whatever most of the Victorians were, they were not at rest. Of course they had their virtues, and most certainly they had their hypocrisies; but the whole point about them was that they were not at rest in either. They still had a religion; but they were always excusing it; explaining it; and very frequently explaining it away. They already had religious doubt; but only in a very few of them was the doubt ever allowed to become denial. The Englishman was patriotic even to excess; but not to the point of ease in excess; like the eighteenth-century farmer who still figures in our caricatures as John Bull. He boasted against foreigners; but he had become conscious of the existence of these horrid little creatures; and the Victorian authors really plagued him with foreigners, like a scourge of locusts or wasps. Carlyle was always throwing Germany at him; Browning was always throwing Italy at him; Matthew Arnold really threw all Europe at him, as if he were the least instructed person in Europe. He did not lose his self-satisfaction; I fear he has not lost it yet. But it was not satisfaction in the sense of security of mind. The Englishman was already puzzled, if only subconsciously, even in the time of Thackeray and Bulwer Lytton; and it seems to me that he has gone on being more and more puzzled ever since.

In short, it was a time of tradition; and most emphatically not a time of stagnation. That is not to say that it might not have been happier in stagnation; but anyhow it was not really happy in transition. It was a very curious mixture of two things; the remains of what had hitherto been a system of Puritanism, with the incessant infiltration of what may be called Romanticism. The notion of summing up half the nineteenth century with the name of Mrs Hemans will be instantly corrected by merely mentioning the name of Mrs Browning. Mrs Browning's verse was never completely strong and it was sometimes decidedly weak; but, whatever it was, it was not prim or pallid or composed of prunes and prisms. Sometimes she rather resembles Victor Hugo in being weak through sheer violence; through straining too much after emotional emphasis or pictorial sensationalism. She was simply one of those Victorians of Puritan origin who were swept away on the flood of the Romantics. Another great woman of the period illustrates exactly the same combination. For this is why *Jane Eyre* remains as a real red-hot testimony to the time; precisely because of the contrast between the prim and prosaic little governess that she was supposed to be, and the wild and almost anarchic emotion that filled her from within. But though I have used the word 'anarchic', it is not the right word; for she was one of those who might break a law but could not ignore it. And she recognized right and wrong, not only because she had been a Puritan; but also because she was a Romantic. That was the point about romanticism, as compared with much modern realism. A fine French critic, M. Mauriac, has said, 'The Romantics were the corrupt children of Christianity.' I should not put it so harshly; but it is very much more true than talking of the Victorians as smug contented Christians. The Victorian Age was really a violent collision and struggle; a meeting-place of two furious onslaughts, but so interlocked and straining, that at this distance from it, it seems to be standing still.

THE NATIONAL SPIRIT

This is written amid fields of snow within a few days of Christmas. And when last I saw snow it was within a few miles of Bethlehem. The coincidence will serve as a symbol of something I have noticed all my life, though it is not very easy to sum up. It is generally the romantic thing that turns out to be the real thing, under the extreme test of realism. It is the sceptical and even rational legend that turns out to be entirely legendary. Everything I had been taught or told led me to regard snow in Bethlehem as a paradox, like snow in Egypt. Every rumour of realism, every indirect form of rationalism, every scientific opinion taken on authority and at third hand, had led me to regard the country where Christ was born solely as a sort of semi-tropical place with nothing but palm-trees and parasols. It was only when I actually looked at it that it looked exactly like a Christmas card. It was only by the sight of my bodily eyes and against all my mental training that I realized how true is the tradition handed down in a Christmas carol. The birth and death of Christ, the whole early Christian drama, did not take place on a flat stage called the desert, covered with sand like a circus and decorated with a few pantomime palm-trees. To begin with the desert is not flat and, to go on with, the Palestinian hills are not the desert. It might well have been far more like the traditional Christmas scene than any of the learned reconstructions that conceive it as a conventional Oriental scene. The whole background was so mountainous as to be in many ways northern. The shepherds were shepherds of the hills as certainly as if they had fed their flocks on the Grampian hills, like the father of Norval. In truth, Palestine is really a strange and symbolic country; and in nothing more than its series of levels and climates. It is not so much a land as a ladder. Degrees of altitude take the place of degrees of latitude. The Jordan Valley really has the atmosphere of those tropics which seem like the suburbs of hell. But the holy mountain of Jerusalem has really an air of something lifted nearer to heaven. It has the clearness and coldness not of being nearer to the poles but of being nearer to the stars.

Now this nameless northern element in the first landscapes of Christianity has had a certain effect on our own history. As the great creed and philosophy which united our fathers swept westward over the world, it found its different parts peculiarly fitted to different places. The men of the Mediterranean had, perhaps, a more intimate sense of the meaning of the imagery of the vine. But it succeeded in making its own imagery equally out of the northern holly and even the heathen mistletoe. And while the Latins more especially preserved the legends about the soldiers, we in the North felt a special link with the legend of the shepherds. We concentrated on Christmas, on the element of winter and the wild hills in the old Christian story. Thus Christmas is, in a special sense, at once European and English. It is European because it appeals to the religion of Europe. It is English because it specializes in those religious customs that can make even our own landscape a holy land.

The tragedy of England is that she has in these things been growing less English. This would be painfully plain if we could discuss these matters in a detached and dispassionate manner, like an abstract question of art. A recognizable and recognized national character in literture and manners appears long before the end of the Middle Ages. Anybody who recognizes that Dickens is English as compared with Balzac, can also recognize that Chaucer is English, as compared with Boccaccio. As to the moment when that national soul was most supreme and secure of itself, there might be differences of opinion. But no serious observer can doubt that it has since lost its security. The fads that so easily become fashions in our own time would be choked with laughter in their very birth, if that spirit were present in its ancient strength. We recognize an Englishman in Chaucer's Franklin in whose house 'it snowed meat and drink'. But he would not recognize an England in which anyone could suggest that it should snow nut cutlets and temperance beverages. He would think he was in a foreign country, not to say another planet.

When we step across the centuries from Chaucer to Dickens we find the same identical snowstorm raging in the Christmas household of Mr Wardle at Dingley Dell. And we recognize, in exactly the same way, and neither more nor less, that Mr Wardle is an Englishman. But though Wardle feels equally secure, Dickens does not feel equally secure. Though the Squire is as comfortable as the Franklin, the modern novelist is not so comfortable as the medieval poet. Dickens is already on the defensive; for he has something to defend. Dickens is not only potentially but positively scornful, for he has something to scorn. The unnatural notions have already begun to eat away the national tradition. Dickens lived to see people proposing to enforce universal teetotalism. If he had survived to see the proposals which some scientific idealists are already drawing up on paper, it may be that his feelings would have been beyond even his own powers

of expression. It may be that the modern world has out-
stripped satire. I doubt whether even Dickens could have
made it funnier than it is.

But the point for the moment is that all this nonsense
is in a special sense the loss of a national spirit. Though
the progress has largely been peculiar to England, it is
none the less a progress away from England. The national
movement has been away from the national idea. It
will be noted that nearly all the greatest Englishmen,
especially the most English Englishmen, were more or
less conscious of this. The other great figures between
Chaucer and Dickens are nearly all figures with their
faces turned to the past. It is what makes men call
Shakespeare monarchical and medieval; it is what made
Johnson a Tory; it is what made Cobbett so singularly
reactionary a Radical. Even the exceptions have exceptional moments when they are conscious of it; a Puritan
like Milton in the rustic reminiscences of 'L'Allegro';
a Whig like Addison in the Christmas ceremonies of Sir
Roger de Coverley. Those Christmas ceremonies, coming
down from a time when Chaucer and his Franklin could
enjoy them, have nevertheless suffered all sorts of damage
from new and less liberal philosophies. They were at-
tacked by the Puritans on theological, by the Utilitarians
on economic, and now by the new Sociologists on
hygienic grounds. The new Scrooge wishes to give everyone else gruel.

A nation may exaggerate itself or fall short of itself;
but a nation must not contradict itself. We should all feel
it if the French were to lose all concern about logic; but
there is a real danger of the English losing all concern
about liberty. There is a real danger that the broad farce
and broad freedom which we feel in Chaucer or Dickens
will actually be less apparent among us than among

foreign peoples which have always had more officialism in their law and more classicism in their literature. The farce is already being thinned by a sort of tenth-rate idealism bearing the detestable American name of 'uplift'. The freedom is already being lost in a network of police prohibition. Between the ideality and the efficiency the English liberty may well be entirely lost. I should not write this if I did not think that it may also be saved. But I could not write it without recording my own conviction that there is only one way of saving it. We have lost our national instincts because we have lost the idea of that Christendom from which the nations came. In freeing ourselves from Christianity we have only freed ourselves from freedom. We shall not now return to a merely heathen hilarity, for the new heathenism is anything but hilarious. If we do not recover Christmas, we shall never recover Yule.

THE RIGHTS OF RITUAL

St Augustine, if I remember right, said, among many other shrewd things about the relation of religious creed to social custom : 'Funeral ceremonies are not a tribute to the dead, but to the living.' It is part of a truth that is constantly forgotten in controversy about ceremonial and symbol. Yet it is a point upon which the Puritan is really less religious than the Pagan. If you had gone up to an ancient Greek in the time of Plato, as he stood offering sacrifice to Athene, you might very well have asked with some curiosity the question about the ancients that has never been quite satisfactorily answered by any of the moderns : 'Do you really believe that the pure goddess of wisdom wishes you to kill or burn something on this particular stone? Does she really require this above all other things?' But the Athenian, if he were as intelligent as most Athenians, might very well answer you by saying : 'Whether or no Athene requires it, I am sure that I require it.' If you went into the household temple of a Chinaman and found him burning pieces of paper to appease his great-grandfather, you might ask him what good his great-grandfather would get by that. But the Chinaman would really have the best of the argument if he answered, 'I do not fully understand the good it does to my great-grandfather, but I do understand the good it does to me.'

To find expression in emblem and established ritual for feelings that are most difficult to express in words is not merely a salute to the departed; it is also a liberating gesture for the living. It is even especially an expression of the life of the living. The practical alternative to it is not speech but silence; not simplicity, but merely embarrassment. Not one man in a thousand ever *says* anything worthy of the dead, or even at all adequate to his own emotions about the dead. It is a far fuller release for his feelings to do something; and especially something that is not too unusual or unnatural to do. The motions that men have always made, uncovering, bowing the head, scattering flowers on the grave, are in the real sense individual actions. They are not only more dignified, but more direct than official speech or extempore prayer. They are not only more serious, but more spontaneous than the ghastly mummery of 'saying a few appropriate words'. A man would be more likely to do such things than to say such things even if he were left entirely to himself, without tradition or culture, even if he were a savage or an utterly unlettered peasant. Ritualism is more natural than rationalism about these things. It is a living necessity for those who survive; sometimes almost a necessity to enable them to survive. It is almost the first gesture of awakening, by which they show that they have not also been struck by the thunderbolt. 'Funeral ceremonies are not a tribute to the dead, but to the living.'

Christmas is a festival of joy and a national funeral is a festival of sorrow; but they both bring in this problem of the present which has always been the practice of the past. And indeed there is more connexion between the two ideas than many suppose, especially of those who are largely out of touch with the present, through being entirely out of touch with the past. For a man without history is almost in the literal sense half-witted. He is only in command of a part even of his own mind.

He does not know what half his own words mean, or what half his own actions signify. And in the great human past there was a profoundly human connexion between days of mourning and days of merriment. The same words were used about both—or, what will seem to some still more strange, the words were interchanged and the phrase that seems to us appropriate to one was specially applied to the other. In ancient times a funeral had many of the elements of a feast. In ancient times a dance could have much of the gravity of a divine service. They used the word 'banquet' about the tragic occasion. They used the word 'solemnity' about the frivolous occasion. Achilles, mourning over Patroclus, summons the heroes to take part in games, as on a school holiday devoted to sports. Theseus in 'A Midsummer Night's Dream', cracking jokes and watching burlesques, at his wedding feast, says : 'A fortnight keep we this solemnity.' And though our civilization has grown in some ways more complex and cannot express these truths with quite the same unconscious sincerity and natural tact, it is well not to forget altogether that our fathers felt this comradeship in their grief and this religion in their merriment.

The ancient world conceived that pagan gods presided over every social function and every activity of daily life; and much of the position that had been given to pagan gods was afterwards very wisely given to patron saints. But there has arisen in modern times a mood that is not so much influenced by pagan gods as by godless paganism. Its funerals are not feasts; and, in a very different sense, its feasts are funerals. The old Christian saint bade men be sorry, not as men without hope. The new pagan sage rather bids them to be merry as men without hope. The frivolity of the pessimists, of the sceptics, and the

K

decadents has been something that connects gaiety with piety by getting rid of both of them. It cannot create any of those symbolic forms of beauty that remain permanent as ritual or even as revelry. Funeral ceremonies are a tribute not to the dead but to the living. But these men are not living; they are of the sort that would scorn equally the little pieties of the poor about mourning, even public mourning, and the traditional games and jokes of a festival like Christmas. Just as they do not understand how much life there is in the cult of the dead, so they do not understand how much truth there is in the repetition of the joke. They are not subtle enough to understand what is simple, nor have they the insight or intelligence to understand the plain and popular things.

The tamest person following tradition is a little more in the main stream of life than that. He may not be an exceptional person, but at least he understands what is meant by an exceptional occasion. He may be a little like a vegetable or a plant that only flowers or comes to life at certain regular seasons. But at least he is not like a stone that never comes to life at all. And the cheap stoic or superior person is none the less as lifeless as a stone, because he generally regards himself as a precious stone and falls into the not uncommon geological error of supposing that he is the only pebble on the beach. Compared with him, there is something like movement in the mere mass of pebbles that are rolled to and fro by the sea.

When, therefore, we watch some popular pomp go by, especially a pomp of lamentation, let us think not only of the virtues of the dead, but of the living; and above all of that universal human virtue of veneration for the dead. Grief is a thing really popular; that fact, if we consider it, will appear very notable and impressive; and when we have understood it we may understand why the great voice that said of old upon the mountain : 'Blessed are the poor,' added but a moment afterwards : 'Blessed are ye that mourn.'

THE INSIDE OF LIFE

THE news that some Europeans have been wrecked on a desert island is gratifying, in so far as it shows that there are still some desert islands for us to be wrecked on. Moreover, it is also interesting because these, the latest facts, also support the oldest stories. For instance, superior critics have often sniffed at the labours of Robinson Crusoe, specifically upon the ground that he depended so much upon stores from the sunken wreck. But these actual people shipwrecked a few weeks ago depended entirely upon them; and yet the critics might not have cared for the billet. A few years ago, when physical science was taken very seriously, a clever boys' book was written, called 'Perseverance Island'. It was written in order to show how 'Robinson Crusoe' ought to have been written. In this story, the wrecked man gained practically nothing from the wreck. He made everything out of the brute materials of the island.

As a matter of fact, of course, it is quite unfair to compare 'Robinson Crusoe' with such boys' books as 'Perseverance Island', or even 'The Swiss Family Robinson', not only because it is much greater literature, but because it is literature with an entirely different aim. To lump it with the others because they all occurred on a desert island is no better than comparing 'Wuthering Heights' with 'Northanger Abbey' because both concern an old country house; or bracketing 'Salem Chapel' with 'Notre Dame de Paris' because they are both about a church. 'Robinson Crusoe' is not a story of adventure;

rather it is a story of the absence of adventure—that is, in the first and best part of it. Twice Crusoe runs away to sea in disobedience, and twice escapes with wreck or other peril; the third time we feel that he is set apart for some strange judgement by God. And the strange judgement is the great central and poetical idea of 'Robinson Crusoe'. It is a visitation not of danger but of a dreadful security. The salvage of Crusoe's goods, the comparative comfort of his life, the natural riches of his island, his human relations with many of the animals— all this is an exquisitely artistic setting for the awful idea of a man whom God has cast out from among men. A mere scurry of adventures would have left Crusoe no time for thinking; and the whole object of the book is to make Crusoe think. It is true that, later in the story, Defoe entangles him with Indians and Spaniards; and for that very reason I think the story loses the naked nobility of its original idea. It is absurd to compare a book like this with ordinary stories about schooners and palm-trees, cutlasses and scalps. It was not an adventurous life but an unadventurous life that was the doom and curse of Crusoe.

But this, perhaps, is wandering from the subject—if there is a subject. Let us try to get back to the desert island and the moral to be drawn from all the happy Australians and their adventure. The first and most important point is this : that when one reads of these forty-five persons tipped out into an empty island in the Pacific, one's first and instantaneous flash of feeling is one of envy. Afterwards one remembers that there would doubtless be inconveniences; that the sun is hot, that awnings give you no shelter until you have put them up; that biscuits and tinned meat might begin to taste monotonous, and that the most adventurous person, having got

on to the island, would before very long begin to turn
his thoughts to the problem of getting off again. But the
fact remains that before all these reflections the soul of
man has said like the snap of a gun, 'How jolly!' I think
this instinct in humanity is somewhat interesting; it may
be worth while to analyse this secret desire to be wrecked
on an island.

The feeling partly arises from an idea which is at the
root of all the arts—the idea of separation. Romance
seeks to divide certain people from the lump of humanity,
as the statue is divided from the lump of marble. We read
a good novel not in order to know more people, but in
order to know fewer. Instead of the humming swarm of
human beings, relatives, customers, servants, postmen,
afternoon callers, tradesmen, strangers who tell us the
time, strangers who remark on the weather, beggars,
waiters, and telegraph-boys—instead of this bewildering human swarm which passes us every day, fiction asks
us to follow one figure (say the postman) consistently
through his ecstasies and agonies. That is what makes one
impatient with that type of pessimistic rebel who is always complaining of the narrowness of his life and de-
manding a larger sphere. Life is too large for us as it is :
we have all too many things to attend to. All true
romance is an attempt to simplify it, to cut it down to
plainer and more pictorial proportions. What dullness
there is in our life arises mostly from its rapidity; people
pass us too quickly to show us their interesting side. By
the end of the week we have talked to a hundred bores;
whereas, if we had stuck to one of them, we might have
found ourselves talking to a new friend, or a humorist,
or a murderer, or a man who had seen a ghost.

I do not believe that there are any ordinary people.
That is, I do not believe that there are any people whose

lives are really humdrum or whose characters are really colourless. But the trouble is that one can so quickly see them all in a lump, like a land surveyor, and it would take so long to see them one by one as they really are, like a great novelist. Looking out of the window, I see a very steep little street, with a row of prim little houses breaking their necks downhill in the most decorous single file. If I were landlord of that street, or a visiting philanthropist making myself objectionable down that street, I could easily take it all in at a glance, sum it all up and say, 'Houses at £40 a year.' But suppose I could be father confessor to that street, how awful and altered it would look! Each house would be sundered from its neighbour as by an earthquake and would stand alone in a wilderness of the soul. I should know that in this house a man was going mad with drink, that in that a man had kept single for a woman, that in the next a woman was on the edge of abysses, that in the next a woman was living an unknown life which might in more devout ages have been gilded in hagiographies and made the fountain of miracles. People talk much of the quarrel between science and religion; but the deepest difference is that the individual is so much bigger than the average, that the inside of life is much larger than the outside.

Often when riding with three or four strangers on the top of an omnibus I have felt a wild impulse to throw the driver off his seat, to drive the omnibus far out into the country and tip them all out into a field, and say, 'We may never meet again in this world; come, let us understand each other.' I do not affirm that the experiment would succeed, but I think the impulse to do it is at the root of all the tradition of the poetry of wrecks and islands.

TRICKS OF MEMORY

THERE are many books which we think we have read when we have not. There are, at least, many that we think we remember when we do not. An original picture, perhaps, was imprinted upon the brain, but it has changed with our own changing minds. We only remember our remembrances. There is many a man who thinks he can recall the works of Swift or of Goldsmith; but, indeed, he himself is the principal author of 'Gulliver's Travels' or 'The Vicar of Wakefield', which he recalls. Macaulay, with his close reading and miraculous memory, was quite certain that the Blatant Beast was killed at the end of 'The Faerie Queene'; but it was not. A brilliant and scholarly friend of mine quoted a stanza as one in which not one word could safely be altered— and quoted it wrong. Hundreds of highly educated people are quite fixed in false versions touching facts that they could easily verify. The editor of a Church newspaper (in rebuking Radicals) asseverated again and again, after contradiction and challenge, that the Catechism commands a child 'to do his duty in that state of life to which it has pleased God to call him'. Of course the Catechism says no such thing, but the editor was so certain that he would not even open his prayer-book to see. Hundreds of people are sure that Milton wrote, 'To-morrow to fresh fields and pastures new'. Hundreds of people are sure that Jesuits preached that the end justifies the means; many of them are sure that they have seen some Jesuit's statement to that effect; but they have not.

But it is a stranger thing still that memory can thus trick us about the main artistic effect of really fine books. Until about a year ago I believed that I had a vivid recollection of 'Robinson Crusoe'. So, indeed, I had, of certain images of the wreck and island; above all of the admirable fact that Crusoe had two swords instead of one. That is one of the touches of the true Defoe; the very inspired poetry of the accidental and the rough-and-tumble; the very romance of the unromantic. But I found I had completely forgotten the really sublime introduction to the tale, which gives it all its spiritual dignity —the narrative of Crusoe's impiety; his two escapes from shipwreck and opportunities for repentance; and, finally, the falling upon him of this strange judgement : food, security, silence—a judgement stranger than death.

With this case in mind I am in no position to exult over my fellow-critics when they prove that they have not read properly the books that, as it happens, I have read properly. But I have been somewhat singularly impressed with the most cultivated and authoritative criticisms of the dramatic version of 'Jekyll and Hyde', in so far as they refer to Stevenson's original romance. Of the play I cannot speak, but with the romance I am very well acquainted, which is more than can be said of those who have lightly and gracefully criticized it on the present occasion. Most of them said that Stevenson was a charming artist but no philosopher; that his inadequacy as a thinker was well represented in the tale of 'Jekyll and Hyde', which they proceeded to describe with the wildest inaccuracy of detail and a complete oblivion of the design. One idea, above all, has established itself firmly in their minds and I daresay in many other people's. They think that in Stevenson's tale Jekyll is the good self and Hyde the bad self; or, in other words, that the protagonist is wholly good when he is Jekyll and wholly bad when he is Hyde.

Now, if Hamlet had killed his uncle in the first act, if Othello had appeared as a *mari complaisant*, it could not have upset the whole point of Shakespeare's story more than this upsets the whole point of Stevenson's story. Stevenson's story has nothing to do with pathological pedantries about 'dual personality'. That was mere machinery; and as he himself seems to have thought, even unfortunate machinery. The business of the powders I think he himself thought clumsy; but he had to make the tale a modern novel and work the transformations by medicine, unless he was prepared to tell it as a primeval fairy-tale and make them by magic. But he did not care a jot about either compared with the mystical idea in the transformation itself; and that had nothing to do with powders or dual personalities, but only with heaven and hell—like 'Robinson Crusoe'.

Stevenson goes out of his way to emphasize the fact that Jekyll, as Jekyll, was by no means perfect but was rather a morally damaged piece of goods. He had 'a sly cast', in spite of his handsome presence; he was nervous and secretive though not ill-natured. Jekyll is not the good man; Jekyll is the ordinary mixed, moderately humane man, whose character has begun to suffer from some evil drug or passion. Now, that which is thus sucking and draining him is the habit of being Hyde; and it is here that the fine moral of Stevenson comes in, a moral as superior as it is opposite to that popularly put into his mouth. So far from preaching that man can be successfully divided into two men, good and evil, he specifically preached that man cannot be so divided, even by monstrosity and miracle; that, even in the extravagant case of Jekyll, the good is still dragged down by the mere existence of the bad. The moral of 'Dr Jekyll and Mr Hyde' is not that man can be cut in two; it is that man cannot be cut in two.

Hyde is the innocence of evil. He stands for the truth (attested by a hundred tales of hypocrites and secret sins) that there is in evil, though not in good, this power of self-isolation, this hardening of the whole exterior, so that a man becomes blind to moral beauties or deaf to pathetic appeals. A man in pursuit of some immoral mania does attain an abominable simplicity of soul; he does act from one motive alone. Therefore he does become like Hyde, or like that blood-curdling figure in Grimm's fairy-tales, 'a little man made of iron'. But the whole of Stevenson's point would have been lost if Jekyll had exhibited the same horrible homogeneity. Precisely because Jekyll, with all his faults, possesses goodness, he possesses also the consciousness of sin, humility. He knows all about Hyde, as angels know about devils. And Stevenson specially points out that this contrast between the blind swiftness of evil and the almost bewildered omniscience of good is not a peculiarity of this strange case, but is true of the permanent problem of your conscience and mine. If I get drunk I shall forget dignity; but if I keep sober I may still desire drink. Virtue has the heavy burden of knowledge; sin has often something of the levity of sinlessness.

THE CODE NAPOLÉON

I

WHILE being what many would call a fanatic for the French alliance, I cannot bring myself to admire the suggestion that we should alter such names as that of Waterloo Station, out of delicacy towards the French. If once the memory of a national victory is to be regarded as an international insult, France herself would have to apologize to nearly every country in Europe. There is scarcely a city on the Continent the French have not entered in triumph; there is scarcely a flag in the civilized world that the French have not hung on their temples or their triumphal arches; there is scarcely a kingdom or a province that has not the name of a French victory that might be or is the name of a Paris street. If such a reminder to the victors is a reproach to the vanquished, England, as well as Europe, has a right to complain of the monuments of France. Every statue of Joan of Arc is a memorial of English defeat. In short, if we, the English, did really desire to glorify the memory of the Battle of Waterloo, it would seem that we have adopted a rather dingy and ineffectual way of doing it. We have never been very fortunate with our public monuments, and Waterloo Station would certainly seem to be one of the least felicitous. The great figure on the Colonne de Vendôme can afford to smile at the artistic effort.

But there is another reform, connected with the same set of ideas, which I would very respectfully urge as a substitute. I fear it is a much more radical and even

146

revolutionary reform than the alteration of a name connected with the defeat of Napoleon. It is that we should leave off talking nonsense about Napoleon, and especially talking nonsense against Napoleon. It is, that instead of bothering about whether a large railway shed is named after the Battle of Waterloo, we should actually try to learn something about the Battle of Waterloo and about the real merits and demerits of the European adventure which finally failed there. So drastic and even dramatic a change in our historical habits is certainly more of an undertaking than the alteration of a luggage label from Waterloo to Stockholm or Brest-Litovsk, or some name which our Pacifists might prefer. Men will certainly not forget Waterloo any more than they will forget Napoleon; and since we cannot forget them, we are almost driven back on the desperate expedient of understanding them.

In looking over a large number of English articles and essays touching Napoleon I was astonished to find how insular and even ignorant our national tradition still is on the subject. So far as moral atmosphere is concerned, nothing seems to have changed. Bonaparte is still Boney; nobody denies his genius now; but nobody denied it then. Even those whose very natural emotions at the moment made them insist that he was a great tyrant, a great murderer, a great monster, did not dispute that he was a great man. But what he was doing, what he was driving at, why he was what he was and what the whole terrific business was all about, none of us seems to have had any notion then, and none of us seems to have any notion now. What is wanted is not glorification of Napoleon, still less glorification of him as a demi-god, which is even worse than denunciation of him as a demon. What is wanted is a calm and candid consideration of

him as a historical human being, and of the things he
stood for, which were much more important than himself.
This is the one thing that nobody will do for Napoleon;
and the trick by which his reasonable fame still suffers is
simple enough.

The trick consists of first artificially attiring him in all
the terrors of a superman, and on that ground denying
him the rights of a man. Somebody said the devil was a
gentleman; and somebody else said that Napoleon was
not a gentleman. The trick consists in expressing surprise
that he was not a gentleman when we have settled to our
own satisfaction that he was the devil. But if we need
sanity touching Napoleon in his personal aspect, we need
it much more in his public aspect. For the things for
which Napoleon really fought were the very contrary
of those cloudy and fatalistic things with which his
legends have been clothed. If ever a man stood for the
strong southern sun against the clouds and the confusing
twilight, it was he. What Napoleon stood for was common sense—*le bon sens français*. That French common
sense can sometimes be cruel, but never fatalistic. It
despises dooms and omens and hereditary curses and
chosen races and all the superstitious necessitarianism of
the North. In short, he stood for French freedom and in
this sense for French free thought. But if there was another thing he stood for, it was French respectability.
He represented a mass of customs and conceptions, of
which his English enemies seemed to know nothing and
his English admirers to know less. His laws cannot be
understood without the French key of domesticity. All
his legislation and social reform revolved round the very
thing which all our legislation and social reform are seeking to destroy—the family. It was the very reverse of
what we call grandmotherly legislation, but it might in

one sense be called legislation for grandmothers. The central figure of its family council was that terrible person the French grandmother. If Napoleon was not always a Christian, he was always a pagan, and what paganism would call a pious pagan. He understood the thing that so many French poets express, the veneration of the soil and the invocation of the dead. In all this he was doubt-less merely the leader of Latin culture; and all the more because all forms of that culture are rooted in the form we call agriculture. It desires the human family to stand on its own feet, within the frontiers of its own land. With that object it was revolutionary. With that object it is conservative. The French Revolution cannot be under-stood, till we realize that it is exactly where the Jacobins went that the Bolshevists cannot follow.

II

Napoleon did once say, among many other random and cynical remarks in a busy life, that he doubted whether he really loved anybody. If human beings in history were treated with half the sympathy and sobriety given to human beings in novels, we should all understand that this was probably the bitter and brief expression of some mood of hardening, common in middle age, but faced with all the realism of a Latin. Napoleon, in early life, had quite certainly loved not wisely but too well. So much for the remark itself. And now let me draw attention to something that went along with it. Imme-diately after Napoleon had said in his haste that he loved nobody, he corrected himself and added as an after-thought some such words as these: 'Except perhaps Joseph, from a sort of habit; because he is the eldest of us.' Now, those who regard Napoleon either as Satan or a Superman would never have dreamed of his saying that. It is the very last thing they would expect him to say; it is the very last exception they would expect him to make. They would understand the sinister hero being faithful to one faithless woman; or worshipping some *Princesse Lointaine* of legendary beauty; or having his weary heart refreshed by a golden-haired child or beggar maid; or taking the advice of some wild prophet or jester in whom anything was tolerated. But that he should still have a humdrum and almost humble attachment to the head of the family, bigger than he in the nursery and the playground, and for no other reason whatever, is an anti-climax to all anarchical romance. The Superman is still actually looking up to his elder brother, simply because he is his elder brother. We look for Napoleon and we find Buonaparte *ainé*. In Thackeray and nearly all English fiction, it is taken for granted, with a laugh, that a fellow can hardly be expected to be very fond of his elder brother. In the Code of the Corsican Ogre it is taken for granted, with entire innocence, that a fellow cannot help being fond of his elder brother, even if it is only a habit. That is what I mean when I say that if we wanted to find the virtues of men like Napoleon we should look for them in the wrong place. That is what I mean when I say that we do not understand even what such a Latin would mean by trying to be good, if he did try to be good. His virtues would startle us by their staleness. The devil would hardly become anything so romantic as a monk; but rather a bourgeois. He would be domestic and almost dowdy.

In short, Napoleon may or may not have had all these fancy virtues and vices of the strong man; but, anyhow, there was something that was stronger than Napoleon. There was something that he served and did not really pretend to rule. He served his own family; and he served the whole institution of the family. Much of the Code Napoléon turns upon it, and its economic expression in a peasantry. It is the supreme and sacred institution of Latin society; and whether we are to be friends or foes of that society, we shall be wise to understand it better. The men who are professing to reconcile all nations do not attempt to understand it at all.

CYRANO AND CHANTECLER

I HEAR that an attack is being made by some of the French critics upon 'Chantecler' and the Rostand reputation generally—an attack taking the form of a charge of 'mere rhetoric' and a protest against extravagant and even insolent puns. That some such hostile impression might exist in England I could well understand. To begin with the simplest reason, the little I have happened to see in the way of English translation of Rostand has been laughably inadequate. I even remember seeing a version of 'Cyrano de Bergerac' in which the last line of the Ballade of the Duel was translated quite literally. As everybody knows, each verse of that impromptu poem ends with the line, 'A la fin de l'envoi je touche'—that is, 'I hit you at the end of the *envoi*', or last verse. Obviously, it should be roughly rendered 'I hit you when the ballad ends' or 'And at the ballad's end the blow', or anything of that kind. In this learned translation, Cyrano was made to say at the end of every stanza, 'And at the envoy's end I touch'. Not one person in ten in an English theatre would know that 'touch' is a French technical term for a hit in fencing. Not one person in twenty would know that the *envoi* is the ritual last verse of the old French ballade. If therefore Cyrano said 'At the envoy's end I touch', it is impossible to conceive what an English crowd would think he meant.

But, of course, this verbal mistranslation is only the emblem of a much deeper sort of misunderstanding. It is no disgrace to an intelligent Englishman of a certain type that he cannot care for Rostand's military brilliancy; just as it would be no disgrace to a classically-minded Frenchman that he could see nothing beautiful in the tangled forest of Browning. There is an English temper in which the violence of French rhetoric seems merely stiff and thin. Such a type of Englishman would be annoyed both ways by a Rostand drama. The nose of Cyrano de Bergerac seems to him as gross as the nose of Ally Sloper. The rhetoric of Cyrano de Bergerac seems to him as artificial as that of Bombastes Furioso. The two spiritual roots of difference lie in two French qualities which the English scarcely possess at all; first the power of feeling that hatred is something holy; and second the power, not merely of laughing at oneself, but of laughing unmercifully. Our English idea of a hero is built upon the sailor, the accessible and open-hearted fellow who kills everybody with the kindest feelings. Our hero is Nelson or Harry V—I mean the genial and magnanimous Henry V of Shakespeare, not the morbid and cruel Henry of history. Nelson wears his heart on his sleeve, as he wears his Orders on his coat. Shakespeare's King Henry broods over his beloved subjects and seeks to give them (in a splendid line) 'a little touch of Harry in the night'. But Cyrano, though he fills the stage, is by no means a universal gentlemen. Cyrano, though he lives and dies for love, is by no means, in the general sense, a loving or a lovable character. It is his vice, he says, to wish everybody to hate him. He compares love to the loose Vandyck collars that are coming into fashion, and hatred to the stiff Elizabethan ruff which he still retains; it is uncomfortable, but it holds a man's head up : 'La Haine est un carcan, mais c'est une auréole.' To be a bitter and exact critic of society, to lash the age, to demand that acting, writing, fencing should reach a severe standard, to wage a lonely war on stupidity—this is a French idea; it is the idea of Rostand's Cyrano, just as it is the idea of Molière's Misanthrope. It is hard for an Englishman (at least, it is hard for me) heartily to like this idealistic cruelty. It is hard for us to imagine scorn as something fruitful and ever-festive; to behold that bitter tree bearing lovely blossoms and delightful fruit. It is hard for us to realize a pageant of blazing wit and romantic activity all produced by such stiff anger as has produced an anchorite or a suicide. It is as if all the gay Athenian comedies had been written by Timon of Athens. But though this sentiment of sacred hate is not easy to us, that is no reason why we should not do justice to it. And France may fairly claim that much philanthropy has been founded by the Misanthrope.

The other un-English quality is best represented in 'Chantecler' itself. The Englishman can laugh at himself, but the Frenchman can sneer at himself, can laugh at himself till himself gets cross. It was very French to parade the fierce satiric poet Cyrano, the very romance of unpopularity, defying human society and taunting death. It was very French to devote a whole tragedy (as in 'L'Aiglon') to the mere memory of Napoleon, the mere size of his shadow. It had the same heroic impossibility as that great Spanish legend in which two knights led out the corpse of the Cid on horseback and all the armies of the Moors fled before it. But it was most French of all, after exhibiting these towering heroes, suddenly to exhibit them again as clucking fowls in a farm-yard and a cock crowing on a dunghill. First, Cyrano's 'panache', his high unbroken feather, brushes the stars; next, it is only the feather of a chicken waddling about a yard. First, Napoleon's trumpet is like the trumpet of the Resurrection, calling to the quick and the dead; next, it is only cock-a-doodle-do from the ragged hero of a hundred cock-fights.

Precisely because Rostand, a romantic and patriotic Frenchman, laughs at the omnipotence of the Gallic cock, many foreigners are enabled to laugh at it who by no means laugh at equally foolish things of their own. The phrase, for instance, that the sun never sets on the British Empire, is quite as intrinsically ludicrous as the idea that the sun cannot rise without the Gallic cock. That measureless, unthinkable furnace which flings its remoter firelight over such stardust as our earth and many like it, is not much more insulted by one idea than by the other. There is mockery in the notion that those awful ancestral fires are encouraged when they hear the cock; there is surely equal mockery in the suggestion that they are discouraged if they do not see the Union Jack. But the difference is that no patriotic English poet will write a romantic drama to point out the cosmic comicality of supposing that the distant and fiery star needs, for its comfort, a little touch of John Bull in the night. But it is French satire that always scores off French heroism; it is the same nation in the two moods; sometimes, as in Rostand's case, it is even the same individual. France has claimed, not without reason, to be the Roman Eagle; she has claimed the eagle and earned it. But she has always gone back on herself to the admission that she is not the eagle, but the cock.

PASSING THROUGH
THE CUSTOMS

THE more a man thinks and travels, the more plainly it will appear that nearly every Christian nation, like nearly every Christian marriage, is a kind of passionate compromise that no one else can understand. Just as in one family the man may collect snakes because he may not smoke cigars, or in another house the woman may be a shrew because she is not a Suffragette, so every great European people achieves a practical equilibrium in some particular and almost secret manner. It is a mistake to suppose that this equilibrium is peculiar to certain people —to talk about Germany as 'efficient', or England as 'businesslike'. In a superficial sense, all the great white nations are efficient; in a deeper and grander sense, the whole human race is as inefficient as an idiot school. But the peoples of Europe are not so much seeking different things as seeking the same things in different ways.

I passed lately through the Custom Houses of three countries—England, France, and Germany. They were as different as a lecture, a massacre, and a morning call; they might have been done in three different planets or by three different races of animals. But they were all equally efficient, they were all a nuisance and they all took almost exactly the same time to a tick of the clock. The French *douane* impressed an English lady who was unfamiliar with travel with the idea that she had got into some particularly squalid and sanguinary corner of the French Revolution. Bullet-headed men barging and banging into everybody, bawling at the top of their voices and throwing luggage about like lumber—this vision struck her simple mind as having in it some element of confusion. She asked how we should ever get to the end of such anarchy. Almost as she said the words the thing was over; everyone had the right luggage, passed with the proper form of examination; everyone was free again and happy. 'These people', I said to her, 'do not bang and bawl because they are confused or lawless, nor because they are inefficient, nor yet because they are efficient. They bang and bawl because they are French; they like it; it seems to soothe them.'

The French Custom House had been a small, dusty, wooden room like a shed. The German Custom House was a vast twilight temple, inlaid with gold and mosaic, like the roof of St Paul's Cathedral. Vast spaces of its echoing floors were not used or even inhabited. Numbers of its officials, standing about in uniforms of an aesthetic peacock green, seemed to have nothing to do at all. There is nothing specially 'practical' about peacock green. One was, indeed, handed about from one official to another and permitted, with silent pomp, to pass from one large waiting-room into another exactly like it. But it was not really oppressive, any more than the French *mêlée* was really brutal; the whole thing was a national sport. And the luggage was inspected and passed, the travellers marshalled and set free, in exactly the same space of time as they had been at Boulogne.

The atmosphere of the English port and Custom House is yet a third thing; less describable, but, I think, even more national than the others. Its spirit is expressed in the English porter; and the nearest definition of the spirit is that it is confidential and comic. Everybody is received off an English boat or train as if he were rather a scapegrace son returning to the family and being met by the old coachman. Even the Custom House officers have a sort of grin. The smell of my country smacked me in the face as I stepped on the Dover Pier. I asked a short, rather beery-looking porter if the train was coming in. He gave an extraordinary sort of roll of the shoulder and jerk of the thumb and said roguishly, 'Yers, Sir; she's comin' in in 'ere . . . ar, she's a-comin' in.' And he went off grinning, as if it were the greatest joke in the world that the ordinary train should come in at the ordinary place. German officials stare at you. French officials scowl at you. English officials wink at you. But they all pass the luggage.

HIS SIGH IS A HULLABALLOO

I BELIEVE our false notion of the French character has been very largely founded on the French cabman. And I believe that being to be a subtle if not sensitive spirit who is much misunderstood. Not all English travellers, perhaps, fall into the merely verbal error of the old lady who observed a certain coldness in the *cocher* whom she had ceremoniously addressed as *cochon*. The type has been better appreciated in that admirable mystery tale, 'Trent's Last Case'. Mr Bentley's hero did justice to the French cabman's cultured vocabulary, safeguarding himself with the remarkable quotation from Keats: 'Happy is England, sweet her artless cabmen; enough their simple loveliness for me.' That deep-minded democrat, Mr Dooley, said that if he were a Frenchman he would be afraid of nobody but the cab-drivers; 'and I wouldn't be afraid of them long, for I'd be a cab-driver meself'. But it has not yet fallen in the way of any social philosopher to analyse the French cabman; if any had done so, he would have destroyed many false ideas about the French citizen.

For instance, the three main impressions formed by the poor old woman about her *cochon* probably were: (1) that he drove wildly; (2) that he shouted, cracked his whip and kicked up a general shindy; (3) that he was rude. The old woman reported this to the other old women who write authoritative books on foreign policy and imperial travel, and the result was a picture of the Frenchman as merely excitable and undisciplined; so that to speak of the French calm still seems like a paradox.

But in truth our old mistake about France falls under three heads which exactly correspond to the three facts mentioned. First, many differences are accidents. They are mentally unfamiliar, but morally colourless. Thus much of the impression of wild driving (though not all) comes from the fact that the rule of the road is reversed and he who is on the right is in the right. This mere unfamiliarity has bred many fictions.

All kinds of jests, criticisms, suggestions of vanity, looseness, stinginess, slackness, gaudiness, have been deduced from the French soldier's red trousers. Even Mr Dooley had a fling at them. But after all there could hardly be a very profound spiritual chasm between the soldier who wore a blue coat with red trousers and the soldier who wore a red coat with blue trousers. Or again, it is a French custom to keep the windows of a restaurant mostly closed. I do not know the reason; very likely there is no reason. But certainly the reason cannot be a cloistered terror of the open air, for the same Frenchman will take his dinner and dinner-table bodily out into the street, at which the English old lady, while untravelled, might possibly faint. A man cannot be hiding behind windows when he can do without walls. Much of the misunderstanding, then, is local custom, like the rule of the road.

Next comes the matter of noise. To some it will seem a paradox, but the noise does not come from the Frenchman being ruffled, but rather from his being unruffled. He has no nerves, as we say when we mean that he has very good ones. His amazing howls do not amaze him. Noise is the normal, like the murmur of breezes or the roll of the distant river. His sigh is a hullaballoo, his whisper a horrible yell. His fathers have followed the cannon in a hundred campaigns and he conducts his daily life like a cannonade. It is true that there mingles with this nervous immunity a touch of fierceness that is not so much emotion as merely impatience. Often it is an intellectual impatience—one might almost say a cold impatience. It is the impatience of a chess-player who cannot be bored with a long game when he already foresees the last move. But this abruptness, sometimes approaching to brutality, has less to do with the noisiness than that other element of invulnerability in the nerves. The streets of Paris do not solely or primarily prove what a racket the French can raise; they prove even more what a racket the French can endure.

And in the matter of politeness, the truth will again appear paradoxical. What makes a poor Frenchman uncivil is the same thing that makes him civil. It is the civil or civic idea—the idea of human equality. Many rich old ladies from more aristocratic countries do really talk as if *cochon* were pretty much the same as *cocher*. If the poor man strikes back it is not to destroy the social structure, but rather to preserve it. He keeps his end up, that the floor may be level. But it is quite true, of course, since human nature is imperfect, that the combination of the democratic instinct I describe with the temperamental impatience I have already noted does produce on occasion an appearance of insolence. This charge against the French is far more well founded than the opposite charge, which it was the fashion of our fathers to bring against them. Indeed, the old stage Frenchman, with his monkeyish excitability, concealed from us the real French defects as much as the real French virtues. We missed the fact, for instance, that the French have some of the harder faults of the Scotch. But, whatever they are, they are not a nation of dancing-masters— rather of cab-drivers.

I am profoundly persuaded that the French are going to lead Europe yet again. Their faults come from being in the core of reality, in the place where things happen. It is their misfortune that they have not the poetry of the islands, the mysticism that comes from living on the edges of things. But they are the better placed for purging democracy of some of the dreamy pedantries into which more exclusive societies have perverted it, and showing what can really be done with liberty, equality, and fraternity. As it happens, the Allies rather specially illustrate that famous trinity. Few have loved liberty so much as the English; none has understood fraternity so well as the Russians. Both have still to grasp the real meaning of equality—that mankind has been made by men.

THE NARROWNESS OF NOVELTY

IT is easy to miss the point of certain modern quarrels, in which I have occasionally intervened; quarrels about things that are labelled Ancient and Modern, like the hymns. Or perhaps, in the case of some of the things, not very like the hymns. Anyhow, the point of the position is this. The real objection to certain novelties is not novelty. It is something that most people do not very much associate with novelty; something which might rather be called narrowness. It is something that fixes the mind on a fashion, until it forgets that it is a fashion. Novelty of this sort narrows the mind, not only by forgetting the past, but also by forgetting the future. There is a certain natural relief and refreshment in altering things, but a wise man will remember that the things that can be altered will be altered again. There is a certain type of Modernist who manages to accept a thing at the same time as fashionable and as final. Indeed, there is a fine shade of difference between something new and something fresh. The former word may be used of something like the New Testament, which is new for ever. But the idea of Something Fresh belongs rather to the exhilarating but less stable world of Mr P. G. Wodehouse.

We pick up a novelty as we pick up a novel; because we think we shall enjoy it, especially if it is a novel by Mr P. G. Wodehouse. But these things are fresh as the flowers of spring are fresh; that is, they are delightful when they come; but we do not disguise from ourselves that they will eventually go. Now it seems to me that much of the modern mind is narrowed by seeing something sacred in the mode or mood of the moment. Thus critics are not content to say that they are not in the mood for Wordsworth or for Tennyson; they talk as if Wordsworth had become worthless, intrinsically and finally worthless, because of the appearance of the stark and ruthless Mr Binks, who does happen to answer at the moment to their mood, and perhaps to the mood of the world. Thus a younger generation, which is now rapidly becoming an older generation, revolted against the Victorian poets, with a sort of illogical logic in their minds; to the effect that they could not really have been poets because they were Victorians. They were not content to say, what is perfectly reasonable, that they were tired of Tennyson. They tried to imply, what is something totally different, that Tennyson is always tiresome. But as between the man who is alleged to be tiresome and the man who is admitted to be tired, there is always the possible inference that he is too tired to enjoy anything. I am not a special worshipper either of Wordsworth or Tennyson; the point is that such merits as they have are unaffected by the accidental nervous fatigue of somebody else. Mr Binks also will some day be a venerable and traditional figure looming out of the past. He also will gain, by respectability and repetition, the formidable power of fatiguing people, and new generations shall rise up and call him tiresome. But surely we cannot admit for a moment that the brilliant—nay, blazing—qualities of Mr Binks, his stabbing actuality, his subservive subconscious attack, his instant vortical violence, his cold incandescence of intellectuality, his death-ray of blank hiatus, his dynamite explosion of dots . . . surely we cannot admit for a moment that our own Mr Binks is worthless, or ever will be worthless, merely because the world will probably pass into some other emotional atmosphere, to which his terrific talents will be less suited; in which his unique type of truth will be less seen; or in which his dazzling but concentrated spotlight will be less on the spot.

Yet these tides and times of mood and fashion are moving even as we talk about them. I have already seen here and there notes written by a new generation, newer than the generation that was tired of Tennyson. I have seen critics beginning once more to praise Tennyson and strangely enough to show a most extraordinary contempt for Swinburne. I do not complain of the change to admiration; I do not even complain of the change to contempt. What I complain of is the shallowness of people who only do things for a change, and then actually talk as if the change were unchangeable. That is the weakness of a purely progressive theory, in literature as in science. The very latest opinion is always infallibly right and always inevitably wrong. It is right because a new generation of young people are tired of things, and wrong because another generation of young people will be tired of them.

I do not call any man imaginative unless he can imagine something different from his own favourite sort of imagery. I do not call any man free unless he can walk backwards as well as forwards. I do not call any man broadminded unless he can include minds that are different from his own normal mind, let alone moods that are different from his own momentary mood. And I do not call any man bold or strong or possessed of stabbing realism or startling actuality unless he is strong enough to resist the merely neurotic effects of his own fatigue, and still see things more or less as they are; big mountains as big, and great poets as great, and remarkable acts and achievements as remarkable, even if other people are bored with them, or even if he is bored with them himself. The preservation of proportion in the mind is the only thing that keeps a man from narrow-mindedness. And a man can preserve the proportion of great things in his mind, even if they do not happen at a particular moment to be tickling his senses or exciting his nerves. Therefore I do not mind the man adoring novelties, but I do object to his adoring novelty. I object to this sort of concentration on the immortal instant, because it narrows the mind, just as gazing at a minute object, coming nearer and nearer, narrows the vision.

What is wanted is the truly godlike imagination which makes all things new, because all things have been new. That would really be something like a new power of the mind. But the modern version of broadening the mind has very little to do with broadening the powers of the mind. It would be a great gift of historical imagination to be able to see everything that has happened as if it were just happening, or just about to happen. This is quite as true of literary as of political history. For literary history is full of revolutions, and we do not realize them unless we realize them as revolutionary. To admire Wordsworth merely as an antiquity is stupid, and to despise Wordsworth as an antiquity is worse than stupid; it is silly. But to admire Wordsworth as a novelty—that would be a real vision and re-creation of the past. For it is solid fact, if any fact be solid, that nearly all the young who were most alert and alive, and eager for a sort of revolutionary refreshment, men like Lamb and Hazlitt and the rest, did feel something in the first fresh gust of the new naturalism; something even in the very baldness and crudity of Wordsworth's rural poetry, which made them feel that he had flung open the gates of freedom more widely than the French Revolution. I do not think it will be any injustice to Mr Binks (always supposing we give him also his proper welcome when he arrives) if we try to understand some of those feelings of our fathers about their favourite authors, and so learn to see those authors as they really ought to be seen. For poets are not stale; it is only critics who are stale; often excusably enough, but even then they need not brag of their own staleness.

THE MERITS OF
SHAKESPEARE'S PLOTS

I SEE that Mr John M. Robertson has written a book about the problem of 'Hamlet', round which the critics still revolve with all the irresolution of which they accuse the hero. I have not read Mr Robertson's book and am thus inhibited by a fine fantastic scruple from reviewing it. But I gather from one of the shrewest and sanest of critics, Mr J. C. Squire, that it explains the inconsistencies of the play as mainly the rugged remains of the old romances or chronicles. It may be suggested that in truth a hero is made human when he is made inconsistent. This is true; but the explanation is at least a great improvement on the insane seriousness of the German psychologists. They talked of Hamlet not merely as a human character but as a historical character. They talked as if he had secrets not only hidden from Shakespeare's readers, but hidden from Shakespeare. This is madness; it is merely staring at a portrait till you think it is alive. It is as if they undertook to tell me the real truth about the private life of Oberon.

Moreover, the case of Hamlet does happen to be one in which Mr Robertson's theory seems relatively right. I should deny any inconsistency in a dreamer doing sudden things like stabbing Polonius; they are just the sort of things a dreamer would do. But it is true that some things out of the old story seem harsh and irrelevant and it is truer still that the old story contains less than usual of the soul of the new story. I say 'less than usual', for I should like to point out that the general rule is rather the other way. Mr Robertson's thesis may be true of 'Hamlet', but it is not so true of Shakespeare.

Of course, much can be said by this time both for and against the national poet. But if it be hopeless to denounce Shakespeare, it may appear almost as impertinent to defend him. And yet there is one point on which he has never been defended. And it is one on which I think he should not only be defended but admired. If I were a Shakespearean student or any kind of student (the improbability of which prospect words wholly fail me to express), I should specialize in the part of Shakespeare that is certainly not Shakespeare. I mean I should plead for the merit of Shakespeare's plots; all the more because they were somebody else's plots. In short, I should say a word for the poet's taste; if only his taste in theft. It is the fashion to abuse Shakespeare as a critic, if only to exalt him the more as a creator. It is the fashion to say that he built on a foundation of mere rubbish and that this lifts to a greater glory the cloud-capped pinnacles he reared upon it. I am not sure that it is such pure praise for a practical architect to say that he was totally indifferent to the basement and cellars, and interested exclusively in the roof and chimney-pots. But, anyhow, I am sure that Shakespeare did not forget the foundation or despise the basement or the cellars.

Shakespeare *enjoyed* the old stories. He enjoyed them as tales are intended to be enjoyed. He liked reading them as a man of imagination and intelligence today likes reading a good adventure story, or still more a good detective story. This is the one possibility that the Shakespearean critics never seem to entertain. Probably they are not simple enough and therefore not imaginative enough to know what that enjoyment is. They cannot read an adventure story or indeed any story. For instance, nearly all the critics apologize, in a prim and priggish manner, for the tale on which turns the Trial Scene in 'The Merchant of Venice'. They explain that poor Shakespeare had taken a barbarous old story and had to make the best of it. As a matter of fact, he had taken an uncommonly good story; one of the best that he could possibly have had to make the best of. It is a clear, pointed, and practical parable against usury; and if a large number of modern people do not appreciate it, it is because a large number of modern people are taught to appreciate and even admire usury. The idea of a man forfeiting part of his body (it might have been an arm or leg) is a highly philosophical satire on unlimited recovery of ruinous debts. The idea is embodied in all those truly Christian laws about wainage and livelihood which were the glory of the Middle Ages. The story is excellent, simply as an anecdote working up to a climax and ending in an unexpected retort. And the end is a truth and not merely a trick. You do prove the falsity of pedantic logic by a *reductio ad absurdum*.

While we have had masses of learned work about the Shakespearean origins, we have had very little about the Shakespearean origin. I mean we have had very little on the main matter of his human and natural inheritance of the whole civilization of Christendom from which he came. It is a commonplace that Shakespeare was a result of the Renaissance; but the Renaissance itself was a result of the Middle Ages; nor was it by any means merely a revolt against the Middle Ages. There are a thousand things in which Shakespeare would be much better understood by Dante than he was by Goethe. I will take one example, all the stronger for being always taken the other way. English patriotism is one of the more manly realities of the modern world; and Shake-speare was a passionate patriot. But in that very passage in praise of England which is hackneyed without ceas-ing to be holy, about half is a medieval memory of the sort called a medieval superstition. It is not about the spacious days of Elizabeth, but the cloistered days of Peter the Hermit. It is not about the Armada but about the Crusades—

> As is the sepulchre in stubborn Jewry
> Of the world's ransom, blessed Mary's Son.

That note was neglected and nearly lost in the whole modern world; and scarcely any modern critic would have cared to notice it. Only the prodigious events of yesterday have brought us back, half-bewildered, into the footsteps of our fathers; and the vision of John of Gaunt was fulfilled in the hour when a great English soldier entered Jerusalem on foot.

A PLEA FOR THE
HEROIC COUPLET

I SHOULD like to see a real poet write again in the heroic couplet of the didactic eighteenth century. Of course (it may be added) we should all like to see a real poet write anything, if he would only do it. But the couplet in question has been under-valued. We have got so used to considering it didactic that we forget that it could be heroic. When the Romantics raised their revolt against the school of Pope, they were probably justified in abandoning it; but they were not justified in representing it as merely neat, still less as merely mechanical. It did lend itself to mere neatness, to the epigram with the sting in the tail. But it was not fair to imply that it was like a Limerick, a thing that could have nothing but a neat ending—a creature that was all tail. It did lend itself to flippancy, as in lines like—

> Die and endow a college or a cat.

It did lend itself to compact contradiction, in lines like—

> And so obliging that he ne'er obliged.

But the notion that it had never done anything but this sort of thing is a fallacy left behind by a forgotten quarrel. Things were written in that restrained metre that have a real epic sublimity. They are not the less imaginative because they left much to the imagination. I use the word epic in the sense that an epic is a sort of gigantic gesture —as when the old French epic was called a *Chanson de*

Geste. It is a deed rather than a word; its very words suggest something beyond them, like a blessing or a blow. Let anyone who can feel the wind and shadow of that mighty movement say whether he does not feel it unmistakably in certain moments of these great poets of the Age of Reason—

> Still raise for good the supplicating voice,
> But leave to heaven the measure and the choice,

in which, to my fancy, the words 'still raise' seem to rise like a lifted hand; or those splendid prophecies of doom—

> Princes and lords may flourish or may fade;
> A breath can make them, as a breath has made

not to mention that deep and indestructible truth for present and future—

> Ill fares the land, to hastening ills a prey,
> Where wealth accumulates and men decay.

These words do not deserve to be condemned as neat. They do not deserve to be despised as witty. We might as well call a speech of Satan or of Samson, as rendered by Milton, merely neat and witty because those who do not appreciate the classic might call it cold. The great gesture may seem to some to be rather that of an orator than an oracle of which the priestess writhes and foams at the mouth in a frenzy; but the same might be said of the speech in Milton. But, even while we agree that a warmer colour or a wilder imagery made more purely poetical the poets before and the poets after Pope, there is no reason why these elements should not enrich the heroic couplet as much as any other metre, or why that which was once used to express reason should not be used again to express imagination. I believe myself that it would be found to be a very full and even a very free form of diction, allowing of a great many good effects old and new, and none the worse if these included among other things the ringing conclusiveness of the printed statement, at once an epic and an epigram.

But whether or no the old form could be used for the highest moods of wisdom, one real advantage attached to it when used for the lower purpose of wit. It did not permit of mystification—nor, therefore, did it permit of mere bluff. There is such a thing as sham wisdom; but there cannot be any such thing as sham wit. There can be a bad pun or a good one; but we do so far see the point that we see the pun. There can be a bad joke or a good one; but we must see the joke even in judging it to be bad. There can be a poor epigram or a powerful one; but we know where to look for the sting, and it is still in the tail. Hence the brain has at least to be at work in some way in order to produce even the worst couplets of the old rationalistic poetry. The brain may be even more magnificently at work in Shelley or Coleridge than in Goldsmith or Pope. But it is much easier to be a sham Shelley than to be a sham Pope. If you want to rival or parody lines like 'Damn with faint praise . . . and without sneering teach the rest to sneer', you must endure for a few moments at least the abnormal agony of thinking. But you can affirm positively that a line you have just written, which runs 'Maniac moonshine sways and staggers,' is quite as good as the line, 'The sanguine sunrise with its meteor eyes' leaping on the back of the cloud, like a large glaring cat, in the lines of Shelley. There is, therefore, no check or limit to the production of purely imaginative poetry—a dark and disturbing thought. Men need only go on repeating that all poetry has been called nonsense, and deducing from this that all nonsense can be called poetry.

One of the thousand things which thinkers of this school never think of is this : that, even if it be true that the old poets were similarly criticized by the yet older critics, the wise man will by no means take it entirely for granted that the older critics were wrong. When we are told, 'We heard the same old-fashioned outcry at the beginning of the Romantic movement,' we shall take the liberty of answering 'Yes; and we have not yet seen the end of the Romantic movement.' If the Romantic movement ends in a mad-house, people will say there was a great deal to be said for those old family physicians, the original classical critics. To most of us, born in the intervening time, it would normally seem natural to prefer the romantic to the rationalistic. We find it difficult to believe that 'Hernani' must be a bad play if it violates the unities of time and place as observed in 'Hecuba'. But if the next play we see preserves the unities by exhibiting as its first scene a section of the interior of the diseased brain of a dipsomaniac, a scene in which all the characters are maggots (or possibly snakes), we shall find ourselves unable to deny that the violation of the unities has in fact led to the violation of the sanities. And if the author of this quiet little idyll of snakes and maggots turns on us scornfully and says, 'The old critics told Victor Hugo the same sort of thing; they told him he was letting in a flood of folly and anarchy to drown the world,' why, there will come upon us a very strong temptation to answer, 'And apparently he was.'

Nevertheless, I do not feel bound to support the old classical critics. I only feel free to support them. That is exactly the difference; and a difference which cannot apparently be made clear to those who talk the cant of

M

novelty. They tell me that they are not to be browbeaten by the established tyrannies of the past. I answer that neither am I to be browbeaten by the successful revolutions of the past. The innovator boasts that he is free to show how time has justified the rebel; but I hold myself equally free to speculate on how a little more time may justify the rebuke to the rebel. Indeed, the rebuke may be justified even when it is not just. I should heartily agree that Keats was a very great man and that Gifford was a very small man. But I might claim the right to defend a small man in the right against a great man in the wrong. The case of Keats is indeed unfair and unrepresentative, which is why it is always taken as typical. Gifford was not merely a small poet or critic; he was a paltry political hack with a personal spite, such as may exist in any age or any school. But if a classical critic said that Keats' early work contained elements capable of dissolving the dignity and severity of poetry, was he wrong? I fancy the admirers of Keats who say so are rather admirers of Keats than readers of Keats. I doubt whether most of them have a habit of reading steadily through 'Endymion'.

When we really welcome the next poet, I doubt whether he will be at all like our notion of the new poet. It may be questioned whether he will really cover the page with sprawling, irregular rhythms or leave it spotted with isolated words and images and symbols. It is quite likely that he will sit down and write in rhymed decasyllabics, or some other old form; and will observe all the old rules and preserve all the old unities—and say all he has to say and hardly know that he has done it.

TO PRAISE, EXALT,
ESTABLISH, AND DEFEND

THERE is a big blank in the cleverest contemporary literature; and it is always difficult to draw a picture of a blank. Nobody finds it easy to define a negative, or to analyse the exact texture of a hole. But I can best begin by quoting certain lines of a friend of mine, not because he is a friend of mine, but because he does give a vivid description of what is not there. Mr Belloc, belonging to older traditions, wrote a Poem in Praise of Wine, of which the first two lines are these—

> To praise, exalt, establish, and defend,
> To welcome home mankind's mysterious friend.

That is the note which, for some reason, has disappeared from most modern writing. There is any amount of sensibility to things, of subtle response to things, of delicate description of how the particular poet is affected by things; but he is never affected in this way. He will tell us that a pool with green scum on it partly depressed and partly delighted him; but he will not *decide*; he will not pronounce upon whether there ought to be any pond; or whether any pond ought to have any scum; or whether any scum ought to be green rather than peacock-blue; or whether, in short, he thanks God for a good green pond, or merely feels inclined to drown himself in it. And as is his aesthetic attitude towards the scum of the pond, so is his moral attitude towards the scum of the population.

He will tell us, to vary the figure, that the glimpse of a girl's mocking face in a crowd left him disturbed and doubtful; but he will not say, as did the great poets of old, that it left him either despairing or resolved. Dante had very little more than a glimpse of Beatrice on this earth; but he instantly perpetuated it in a perspective as solid as architecture, stretching away into the corridors and halls of heaven. Some great poets in the past, when the girl's mocking face was a little too mocking, hardened and fixed and fossilized the memory in exactly the opposite fashion. Catullus came to a very harsh and savage and ungentlemanly conclusion about Lesbia; but he came to a conclusion. There was something in the whole tremendous tradition of the great tragic and comic poets of the past, which tended of its nature to be monumental. Dante set up a stone over Beatrice and Catullus threw a stone at Lesbia; but they were both big stones and they have remained upon the graves. Both felt sure that their gesture was final; and that it really represented what they felt. The very sound of song, the very nature of the opening phrase, was something like that; 'To praise, exalt, establish, and defend'. Or else it was, 'To curse, confound, destroy, and leave for dead'. But that full-throated and final utterance is somehow lacking amid the many and varied voices of modern self-expression, though they claim to have an unprecedented liberty and often do, in fact, have an almost intolerable anarchy. That is the one limit that is really, though silently recognized in current culture and philosophy; and not even the most thoughtful obscenity, or the most fastidious form of madness, can be altogether a substitute for that fullness of life and that firmness of language. It is the new orthodoxy that a man may be uncertain of everything; so long as he is not certain of anything.

I have taken a text from a particular poem; because it so happens that the very terms of that text cover almost every point in the particular case. I will even take those terms in turn, in order to show exactly what I mean. The first words are, 'To praise'. Men have praised all sorts of worthy and unworthy things; they have praised God and golden calves and gold-diggers; tyrants and trivial fops and fashionable leaders; and women dead, like Beatrice, or false, like Lesbia. But even if this praise was false as the lady, it always took on the tone of true and triumphant praise; it always tried to blow the trumpet, though it were the brazen and not the golden trumpet. But the modern poet, though not wholly unaware of his own existence, has not the breath to blow a trumpet; not even his own trumpet. The very noises that come from his musical instrument are of a wavering and inconclusive sort; and if the trumpet give an uncertain sound, who shall prepare himself for the battle? For that matter, even the trumpets of the most triumphant wedding march fail to make that sort of person prepare himself for the wedding. It is a very queer feature of current poetry that there is hardly anywhere such a thing as a love poem; though there is really rather too much poetry about love. The truth is that the poetry is not really about love, or even about lust. It is about something that they call Sex, which is considered from the outside rather than the inside, being at best a subject rather for science than for literature. At the best, they produce a certain amount of psychology, even when it is not psychopathy; and psychology is not poetry.

The second term, 'exalt' is equally essential, but rather more mystical. It is concerned with a process that has accompanied praise, whenever it was great enough to be also poetry. It is connected with the idea of lifting a thing on to a plane in some way analogous at least to that of sacred things. This was the secret of a certain heroic quality in more primitive forms of patriotism. It is not altogether a legend that the patriotism of the City States of Antiquity was a statelier sort of business than the patriotism of the Industrial City of modern times. And the reason was that the heroes were not only praising themselves; they were not even praising only the City; they were praising the gods of the City. That is very different from the modern tribal pride, according to which all the citizens are gods. The modern clerk or stockbroker, who is 'something in the City', may be very patriotic and read a very patriotic newspaper. But he does not praise the gods of the City, he would have some difficulty in finding any gods in the City to praise. The real danger of that parody of patriotism, is that the patriots themselves are supposed to be gods. To all real praise must be added something of that exaltation of the thing worshipped, which is also separation and withdrawal.

But if we insist on the word 'exalt', we must equally insist on the word 'establish'. There seems to be a crazy tradition from the Byronic or Bohemian culture, that poetry must be revolutionary in the sense of destructive. It would seem obvious that poetry can only be creative. But poetry can also be, in a way of its own, constructive. The lover wishes to establish what he loves; whether to establish a woman in a household, or a just law in a city, or a type of life or landscape which he wishes to see endure; but his attitude must be one not of doubt but of demand. The poet is by derivation the Maker, and wishes, not only to imagine but to make.

Lastly, it is only fair to say, even for the poor distracted patriots of these distracting days, that all this will be utterly meaningless, unless modern morality can bring itself to add to it the ringing and decisive word 'defend'. That is where so much of the Pacifist argument never ends, because it never begins. Multitudes of modern men unconsciously shirk the perfectly obvious point that, whatever they want to do, they cannot do it unless they are ready to defend it. You cannot have any ideal, whether political or poetical, without wanting to 'establish' it; and the moment you establish it, somebody else can make you defend it. 'To praise, exalt, establish, and defend'; I do not apologize for repeating the words; for they are much needed in these times.

ON THE TRUE ARTIST

IT has lately been noted that the artists who started with entirely new artistic methods have now themselves returned to more realistic methods, and what some would call more reasonable methods. According to the pioneer theory of progress, of which we have all heard so much, they ought by this time to have shot far out of sight, and be enjoying the society of our great-great-grandchildren. For it is supposed to be the duty of this singular sort of pioneer to lose sight entirely of the army which he leads.

Of course, the whole metaphor is a muddle; most of that modern theory of progress is a muddle of metaphors. A pioneer does not lead an army; he is merely a man who walks in front of it and is as much under the orders of the general command as the last man who walks behind it. But, accepting the vague imagery of those who talk of a pioneer when they mean a prophet, it is clear that the pioneer sometimes falls back on the main body of the advance. In other words, the prophet sometimes gets tired of the society of the babe unborn (who may be an uncommunicative companion) and seeks for companions even among contemporaries. I cannot pronounce upon the case of pictorial art, but in the parallel case of literature there is perhaps something to be said about the tests of such a return to society, and of whether and when it is a return to sanity.

The first truth involved is a truism, but a truism often as little understood as any mystery. It is that the artist is a person who communicates something. He may com-

municate it more or less easily and quickly; he may com-
municate it to a larger or smaller number of people. But
it is a question of communication and not merely of what
some people call expression. Or rather, strictly speaking,
unless it is communication it is not expression. I know
that for some time past it has been the custom to talk of
the artist expressing something as if it only meant his
getting rid of something. It may be natural that the artist
should want to get rid of his art; especially when we
consider what it is sometimes like. But it is not his business only to deliver himself; It is, I say very solemnly, his
business to deliver the goods. This, as I say, is a truism,
but it is one that is strangely forgotten in a great deal
of the fashionable fuss about artistic self-expression. The
artist does ultimately exhibit himself as being intelligent
by being intelligible. I do not say by being easy to understand, but certainly by being understood.

Yet there is still a vast amount of talk about the
isolated and incommunicable spirit of the man of genius;
about how he has in him things too deep for expression
and too subtle to be subject to general criticism. I say that
that is exactly what is *not* true of the artist. That is
exactly what is true of the ordinary man who is not an
artist. That is exactly what is true of the man who is
called a Philistine. *He* has subtleties in his soul which he
cannot describe; *he* has secrets of emotion which he can
never show to the public. He it is who dies with all his
music in him. But it should obviously be the aim of the
musician to die with all his music out of him; even if this
ideal state of things can seldom be achieved.

The point is here, however, that it is not enough that
the musician should get his music out of him. It is also
his business to get his music into somebody else. We
should all be reasonable enough to recognize that the

somebody else will depend to some extent on the sort of music. But if all he can say is that he has a secret of sealed-up power and passion, that his imagination is visited by visions of which the world knows nothing, that he is conscious of a point of view which is wholly his own and is not expressed in anything common or comprehensible—then he is simply saying that he is *not* an artist, and there is an end of it.

The real truth to be recognized on the other side is this. The expression of a unique point of view, so that somebody else shall share it, is a very difficult and delicate matter. It will probably take the artist some time, and a number of experiments, to make his meaning clear. And it seems to me that the moment when he returns to a more normal style is, very often, simply the moment when he has managed to make it clear. The time when he is wild and revolutionary and unfathomable and ferociously original is the time when he is trying to do it. The time when he is called ordinary is the time when he has done it.

It is true that there is a sort of bad parody of this good process. There generally is of all good processes; *diabolus simius Dei*. It does sometimes happen that a man who had revolutionary ideals in his youth sells them for a merely snobbish conformity. But I do not think this is true of the modern artists whose return to a more normal manner has recently been remarked in this connexion. Their work has still an individual character, even when it becomes intelligible as well as individual.

I am only pointing out that the moment when artists become intelligible is the moment when they become truly and triumphantly individual. It is the time when the individual first appears in the world with which art is concerned; the world of receptivity and appreciation.

Every individual is an individual; and I am one of those who think that every individual is an interesting individual. But, anyhow, there are a very large number of individuals who would be interesting if they had the power of arousing our interest. But the moment of creation is the moment of communication. It is when the work has passed from mind to mind that it becomes a work of art.

ON THE ESSAY

THERE are dark and morbid moods in which I am tempted to feel that Evil re-entered the world in the form of Essays. The Essay is like the Serpent, smooth and graceful and easy of movement, also wavering or wandering. Besides, I suppose that the very word Essay had the original meaning of 'trying it on'. The serpent was in every sense of the word tentative. The tempter is always feeling his way, and finding out how much other people will stand. That misleading air of irresponsibility about the Essay is very disarming though appearing to be disarmed. But the serpent can strike without claws as it can run without legs. It is the emblem of all those arts which are elusive, evasive, impressionistic, and shading away from tint to tint. I suppose that the Essay, so far as England at least is concerned, was almost invented by Francis Bacon. I can well believe it. I always thought he was the villain of English history.

It may be well to explain that I do not really regard all Essayists as wicked men. I have myself been an essayist; or tried to be an essayist; or pretended to be an essayist. Nor do I in the least dislike essays. I take perhaps my greatest literary pleasure in reading them; after such really serious necessities of the intellect as detective stories and tracts written by madmen. There is no better reading in the world than some contemporary essays, like those of Mr E. V. Lucas or Mr Robert Lynd. If I may myself imitate the timid and tentative tone of the true essayist, I will confine myself to saying that there is something in what I say : there is really an element in modern letters which is at once indefinite and dangerous.

What I mean is this. The distinction between certain old forms and certain relatively recent forms of literature is that the old were limited by a logical purpose. The Drama and the Sonnet were of the old kind; the Essay and the Novel are of the new. If a sonnet breaks out of the sonnet form, it ceases to be a sonnet. It may become a wild and inspiring specimen of free verse; but you do not have to call it a sonnet because you have nothing else to call it. But in the case of the new sort of novel, you do very often have to call it a novel because you have nothing else to call it. It is sometimes called a novel when it is hardly even a narrative. There is nothing to test or define it, except that it is not spaced like an epic poem, and often has even less of a story. The same applies to the apparently attractive leisure and liberty of the essay. By its very nature it does not exactly explain what it is trying to do and thus escapes a decisive judgement about whether it has really done it. But in the case of the essay there is a practical peril; precisely because it deals so often with theoretical matters. It is always dealing with theoretical matters without the responsibility of being theoretical or of propounding a theory.

For instance, there is any amount of sense and non-sense talked both for and against what is called medievalism. There is also any amount of sense and non-sense talked for and against what is called modernism. I have occasionally tried to talk a little of the sense, with the result that I have been generally credited with all the nonsense. But if a man wanted one real and rational test, which really does distinguish the medieval from the modern mood, it might be stated thus. The medieval man thought in terms of the Thesis, where the modern man thinks in terms of the Essay. It would be unfair, perhaps, to say that the modern man only essays to think —or, in other words, makes a desperate attempt to think. But it would be true to say that the modern man often only essays, or attempts, to come to a conclusion. Whereas the medieval man hardly thought it worth while to think at all, unless he could come to a conclusion. That is why he took a definite thing called a Thesis, and proposed to prove it. That is why Martin Luther, a very medieval man in most ways, nailed up on the door the thesis he proposed to prove. Many people suppose that he was doing something revolutionary and even modernist in doing this. In fact, he was doing exactly what all the other medieval students and doctors had done ever since the twilight of the Dark Ages. If the really modern Modernist attempted to do it, he would probably find that he had never arranged his thoughts in the form of theses at all. Well, it is quite an error to suppose, so far as I am concerned, that it is any question of restoring the rigid apparatus of the medieval system. But I do think that the Essay has wandered too far away from the Thesis.

There is a sort of irrational and indefensible quality in many of the most brilliant phrases of the most beautiful essays. There is no essayist I enjoy more than Stevenson; there is probably no man now alive who admires Stevenson more than I. But if we take some favourite and frequently quoted sentence, such as 'To travel hopefully is better than to arrive', we shall see that it gives a loophole for every sort of sophistry and unreason. If it could be stated as a thesis, it could not be defended as a thought. A man would not travel hopefully at all, if he thought that the goal would be disappointing as compared with the travels. It is tenable that travel is the more enjoyable; but in that case it cannot be called hopeful. For the traveller is here presumed to hope for the end of travel, not merely for its continuance.

Now, of course, I do not mean that pleasant paradoxes of this sort have not a place in literature; and because of them the essay has a place in literature. There is room for the merely idle and wandering essayist, as for the merely idle and wandering traveller. The trouble is that the essayists have become the only ethical philosophers. The wandering thinkers have become the wandering preachers, and our only substitute for preaching friars. And whether our system is to be materialist or moralist, or sceptical or transcendental, we need more of a system than that. After a certain amount of wandering the mind wants either to get there or to go home. It is one thing to travel hopefully, and say half in jest that it is better than to arrive. It is another thing to travel hopelessly, because you know you will never arrive.

I was struck by the same tendency in re-reading some of the best essays ever written, which were especially enjoyed by Stevenson—the essays of Hazlitt. 'You can live like a gentleman on Hazlitt's ideas,' as Mr Augustine Birrell truly remarked : but even in these we see the beginning of this inconsistent and irresponsible temper. For instance, Hazlitt was a Radical and constantly railed at Tories for not trusting men or mobs. I think it was he who lectured Walter Scott for so small a matter as making the medieval mob in 'Ivanhoe' jeer ungenerously at the retreat of the Templars. Anyhow, from any number of passages, one would infer that Hazlitt offered himself as a friend of the people. But he offered himself most furiously as an enemy of the Public. When he began to write about the Public, he described exactly the same many-headed monster of ignorance and cowardice and cruelty which the worst Tories called the Mob.

Now, if Hazlitt had been obliged to set forth his thoughts on Democracy in the theses of a medieval schoolman, he would have had to think much more clearly and make up his mind much more decisively. I will leave the last word with the essayist; and admit that I am not sure whether he would have written such good essays.